The People's H

Pit Boy

Memories of a life in Murton
during the 1930s and '40s

by

P.J. McPartland

An early view of Murton Village.

Culture & Leisure

Copyright P.J. McPartland 2005

First published in 2005 by

The People's History Ltd
Suite 1, Byron House
Seaham Grange Business Park, Seaham
County Durham SR7 0PY

ISBN: 1 902527 90 9

Contents

Acknowledgements

I owe a debt of gratitude extending to several people; family members especially rendered valuable assistance during the various stages of the preparation of the typescript, when I was struggling to cope with the complexities of a word processor. My daughter, Joanne, particularly, gave unstintingly of her time, and to her is due most of the credit for the solution of my difficulties and the preservation of my sanity. My thanks also go to my daughter, Colette for agreeing to read the finished typescript, and for her encouraging remarks. To Andrew Clark of The People's History I extend my warmest appreciation for his unwavering enthusiasm for the project.

Mr M.J. Ridley of Houghton-le-Spring was able to identify the World War II aircraft which crashed on the edge of Murton in 1944 (see chapter four), and also provided me with much interesting information concerning this incident, for which I am most grateful.

For the loan of photographs, I give thanks to Eric and Ann Richardson, Elaine Sampson, Cath Jacques, George Nairn, Jack Hair, Trevor Williamson, J.N. Pace, Annie Purvis, Mollie Coxon, Gerard Short, Kevin Bartley, Mary Coxon, Murton Local History Resource Centre, Bernard Morris and Alf and Margaret Scales. Certain material scattered throughout chapters four, five and eleven first appeared in an article of mine written for Northeast Press Ltd, and published in the Sunderland Echo; it is reproduced here by kind permission of the Editor.

While memory has served me well, it is no more than a fallible guide, and certain persons who feature in the book in a minor capacity have been given fictitious names.

My grandchildren like to be told stories of the 'old days', so it is with much love that I dedicate the book to them, and also to Maureen, who likes life stories.

A TOC H function in the Wesleyan Hall in Murton. Eric Richardson is on the right between his mother, Lily and Grandfather, Fred Myton. Albert Williams is front left.

FROM THE MELTING POT

Blacksmiths at Murton Colliery in the late 19th century. They are typical of the hardy and hardworking folk of the Durham coalfield.

Two historic events took place in England in 1937: Sunderland won the FA Cup for the first time and George VI was crowned king, in that order of importance.

I was born in February of that year; prematurely, so I've been told. Had the prognostication been confirmed by the fact, I might have had the same birthday as Einstein or Ibsen or Alexander Graham Bell, instead of sharing one with gangster Bugsy Siegel and someone who crossed Niagara Falls on a tightrope while pushing a wheelbarrow.

I have no wish to dwell unduly on the matter of my birth, merely observing that, for the purpose of this record, the significance of it derives from the circumstances no less than from the event itself. I particularly mean the circumstance of place, and of the way of life of the people associated with it. The place was the North East of England; the way of life was that of a community that owed its existence to coal. That way of life has now gone, almost completely, and certainly forever.

My paternal grandmother came from English Protestant stock; all other family lines, paternal and maternal, can be traced to Irish Catholic immigrants who came over in the middle of the 19th century in the aftermath of the Famine and to find work in the industrial North East. Both branches of the family eventually settled in Murton, a colliery village eight miles south of Sunderland and two and a half miles inland from the North Sea.

Murton typified the Durham pit community that came into being with the sinking of the deep pits beneath the magnesium limestone, beginning early in the 19th century. The work force was mixed; yet from the melting pot of Irish, Scottish, Cornish, indigenous North

Sunderland captain Raich Carter receives the FA Cup from the Queen.

Easterners and others came something unique, a hardy and hardworking people of cheerful disposition and uncompromising loyalties, whose traditions became enshrined in folklore.

The first colliery houses were stone-built and quickly knocked together on the south side, a stone's throw from the pit shaft. They were given unimaginative, perfunctory names like Murton Street and Durham Place, the latter acquiring the equally unimaginative, if pragmatic, epithet of Sinker's Row. Durham Place also bore the dubious distinction of being the domicile of the poisoner, Mary Ann Cotton, who grew up and went to school in Murton, and whose father, a sinker, lost his life when he fell down the pit shaft.

Murton Street – one of the earliest streets in the village.

In the 1870s, an ambitious building programme was undertaken with the construction of about a dozen rows of tied cottages on the north side of the pit. The streets had pebbled paving and ceramic gutters, and were widely spaced, with outside ornamental water taps and water closets or netties. Owing to an early Cornish connection with the colliery, these terraced streets became known collectively as Cornwall. The area might just as well have been called Ireland, for probably as many people of Irish extraction than Cornish lived there. At the turn of century, much private building had gone on at some small distance south west of the pit. It was here, in a rented, terraced house in Coronation Street West, that I grew up and went to school during the war and the immediate post-war years.

Murton Colliery – a busy scene at bank.

It was a quite ordinary house, with fashionable 1930s furniture and linoleum-covered floors. The front room was carpeted and the kitchen spread with geometrically-designed clippie mats made by my grandmother. The front room was rarely used but we had to go through it to get upstairs. A very small patch of garden with a privet hedge and lily of the valley bordering the edge of the path graced the front of the house. The only lavatory was across the yard at the back, sandwiched between the coalhouse and the washhouse. My bedroom overlooked the yard, and beneath my bedroom was the kitchen, which was the most lived-in room in the house.

It was my mother who ensured that I left the house in good time for school. Breakfast was an unhurried meal of tea and slices of bread and dripping sprinkled with salt, and was eaten at the kitchen table. The dripping was left over from the Sunday joint, which thus provided a breakfast for the rest of the week that was simple, economical and nutritious.

Being conscientious parents, Mam and Dad were concerned that their children should grow up healthy. Fat was then considered essential for good health, and I was frequently scolded for not eating the fat off the meat. Dad would stop what he was doing to glower at me, as with surgical precision I would separate the fat from the meat and push it towards the edge of my plate. 'Don't play around with it. Get it eaten!' finally he would exclaim in exasperation.

Mam thought fat would provide insulation against the winter cold. 'You should eat it, Pat, it will put meat on your bones.' Being of slender build herself, Mam hardly epitomised her own philosophy. Every morning, my younger brother, Joseph, and myself were given our Welfare orange juice, and night and morning we took our teaspoonful of cod liver oil, grimacing as it went down, followed by a generous dessertspoon of either Virol or Numol, malt extracts which were as pleasant to the taste as the cod liver oil was wretched.

Once I started school, I had to get up at eight, however, if it was my week to serve Mass, then I would be called at seven. Mam and Dad were both devout Catholics; they therefore felt honoured when the parish priest, Fr Conway called at the house to request me for one of his altar boys. My cousin, John Morris, who was then in his twenties and a senior altar server, came to the house to coach me in the Latin responses, and from the age of seven until I left school at fifteen I served Mass in church every alternate week before the school day began. Getting up that extra hour early was especially hard throughout the terrible winter of 1947, when we were snowed in every day and Mam and I together had to dig our way out the back door.

The division of labour in mining households was clear-cut and by and large worked well. The husband was the wage-earner, and his responsibility generally ended there. His wife paid the bills and ran the home. So most men, like my father, handed their wages over and took pocket money.

The kitchen was the woman's domain, where a male presence was not always welcome, especially when meals were being prepared. Indeed, there were men who were afraid to enter it uninvited; the fear of a sharp and admonishing tongue was enough to keep them well out of the way. Dad was never banished from the kitchen; he did his share of the washing-up, and on Sunday he rolled his sleeves up to peel or scrape the potatoes for

An advert for Seven Seas Cod Liver Oil.

Sunday dinner, and Mam was grateful for his help.

If the pitman's life was hard, the pitman's wife had it no less easy. Windows had to be cleaned, carpets beaten, brasses polished, steps scrubbed, and the yard regularly swilled and broomed. Then the kitchen range had to be black-leaded weekly. This was a dirty job, which my mother did on her knees, with her sleeves rolled up and her dark hair tucked in beneath her turban.

Before the appearance of washing machines, the weekly wash was probably the housewife's most demanding task, for then it had to be done in the poss tub, where it was vigorously possed with the poss stick. Calling this instrument a stick was a cruel irony. It was much like the trunk of a medium-sized tree, thick and rounded at one end, with a cross-piece inserted through the narrow end to

An advert for kitchen ranges from the 1930s.

form a handle. Once the clothes were judged to have been sufficiently possed so as to render them thoroughly clean, they would be put through the rollers of a hand-operated mangle, before being roughly folded and dropped into a wicker basket beneath the mangle.

Dad did jobs around the house, like filling the coal pails and chopping sticks for the fire. He cobbled all our footwear on his last, fitting new soles and heels to worn boots and nailing segs to new ones so they would last longer.

Once he sent away for hair-cutting clippers, the manually-operated type, not with any thought for economy, but because he rather fancied himself as a barber. Lots of men tried their hand at hair-cutting, and many a back yard served as a barber shop.

Dad's new acquisition, I rightly suspected, was bad news for me. 'Haway, Pat, Aa'll cut your hair,' said Dad eagerly, as for the first time he took the hair-cutting clippers from their box and prepared to use them.

I knew a moment of dread. 'It doesn't need cuttin'.'

'Doesn't need cuttin',' Dad scoffed at the idea. 'It's thick at the back, man. It'll soon be over your collar.'

It was futile to argue. So the clippy mat was rolled back and a stool set on the canvas floor of the kitchen; then an old curtain was draped around my neck and shoulders and tucked in at the neck.

Dad was neither especially skilful in his use of the clippers nor very considerate of my pain threshold. Frequent painful nips from this instrument resulted in a series of red blotches on the back of the neck. When, unable to control my reflex system, I flinched, I was gruffly told to 'Keep still!' However, Mam was on hand for moral support. Arms folded, she looked on with mounting concern, a frown gathering on her brow, as Dad burrowed into the back of my neck with the clippers, periodically twisting my head to the required angle.

'Jimmy, be careful, you're hurting him,' she remonstrated.

Dad stopped for a moment to glare at her. 'Hinney, Aa'm barely touchin 'im.'

But Mam persisted. 'You are. He keeps jumping; he wouldn't jump for nothing.'

Stung by the criticism, and perhaps not a little hurt that his efforts should have gone unappreciated, Dad managed to deflect the blame on to me.

'If he'd of kept his head still Aa'd be finished by now. How do you expect me to cut hair if he keeps movin' 'is head?'

Mam sighed audibly. 'Well, I wish you wouldn't be so rough, Jimmy. His neck's all red – you should see it.'

So with Dad turning a deaf ear to all reasonable entreaties respecting my discomfit, and Mam tut-tutting away in the background, I sat in rigid anticipation of the next and every subsequent assault of the clippers until the ordeal was over.

Dad was not a very demonstrative parent. But if he found outward displays of affection embarrassing, he showed his affection in other ways. I relied on Dad for the manufacture of catapults, bows and arrows, matchstick guns, all the homemade weaponry then in favour. Dad was of less than average height, but well built. Many thought he had been a boxer as he had a flattened nose. He completely lacked a sense of smell. He was fond of walking, and before I started school he took me with him on his walks in and around Murton.

One of our walks took us half-a-mile east along the road out of Murton to the small community of Cold Hesledon, where a man who was marras with Dad lived. A marra was a workmate underground. By extension, the word came to mean friend or acquaintance, and in this latter sense was widely used as an everyday form of address among men. Mr Thomas was both a workmate and a friend. He had a greenhouse where he grew tomatoes, and I liked going there because he gave me the little ones to taste, the little ones being the sweetest.

Cold Hesledon was a place name rarely used in everyday speech; it was the site of a waterworks, and people who lived there were said to live at the Waterworks. There were only about five streets of houses, but the Waterworks had its own school, workingmen's club, and a branch of the Co-op Store. Although it was only a two-penny bus ride to and from the Waterworks, many preferred to walk the distance, particularly in the summer months, when it was a regular sight to see people strolling in both directions. An unusual feature of the Waterworks road was the aerial ropeway that crossed it, carrying the buckets of waste from the pit on one side of the road to the slag heap on the other side. You had to walk beneath a broad net that was strung out between the pylons on both sides of the road and beneath the ropeway high above. This was to catch any fallout from the buckets; but we were so used to this structure being there we hardly noticed it. Parents warned their children of the dangers of playing near the pit heap; Mam never tired of repeating the story of how one boy had disappeared under the slag when playing there.

Sometimes on our walks Dad and I stopped off at places of dubious edification. I was introduced to snooker before I was introduced to the alphabet, as the Billiard Hall was one such stopping-off place. Here, in an atmosphere of half-light and shadows and the inevitable pall of cigarette smoke, amidst the contrasting glare cast by illuminated tables, men in shirt sleeves and waistcoats concentrated their efforts on the green baize. High seating abutted the walls on three sides, enabling the spectators to have a clear view of the tables; and here I perched, a captivated, if unenlightened, onlooker, side by side with Dad, legs dangling above the concrete floor.

At other times, I accompanied him to the Colliery Welfare Park, on the edge of Murton, passing by the cricket ground and the football ground, the seldom-used tennis courts and the never-to-be-used bandstand, where the card schools flourished and shabbily-dressed men engaged in pitch-and-toss. We never lingered here but hurried on by. Dad liked to bet small amounts of his pocket money on horses, but otherwise he never gambled. He deplored the prodigality of men who put their families at risk by gambling their wages.

Weekday mornings were occupied with the business of getting me out of the house in time for school. On Saturdays, however, I was allowed to indulge in the lazy habit of lying late. Instead of being roused from my bed by the urgent tones of my mother's voice, I could expect an unhurried awakening, often occasioned by the sound of some routine activity taking place outside, like the recurrent thwack of someone energetically beating a carpet, or the slow clip clop of horses hooves on concrete.

Although motor transport had been in existence for half-a-century, the pit village still had some catching up to do in that respect and horse-drawn vehicles were the rule. It sounds improbably archaic, but even the dustcart was horse-drawn. It was a high-sided vehicle with a single pair of outsize rubber wheels. Always the same shaggy draught horse pulled it; and always the same two dustmen walked behind it, effortlessly hoisting the aluminium bins on to their shoulders, before depositing their contents into the cart. The bigger of the two men had a hook on the end of one arm, which he used with great dexterity on the bin handle. Dad, who knew him slightly, said that he had lost his hand in the Great War.

The Co-op Store had carts on the street at all times of the day, so it was almost impossible to walk the streets without seeing one. Pre-arranged orders were delivered to the door on the expected day by the grocery cart, while the unmistakeable clanking of pots and pans and aluminium pails announced the approach of the hardware cart. In addition, there was a bread cart, a butcher's cart and a fruit and veg cart. The Store also delivered milk; the number and colour of milk disks left with the empties told the milkman how many bottles to leave and whether to leave pints or halves. In our house we took two pints, so two yellow disks were put in one of the empty bottles last thing at night. For those who preferred the extra creaminess as it came straight from the cow, milk was conveyed direct from the local dairy farm and ladled into jugs from the milk churn.

Competing with the Store in the fruit and veg business were independent tradesmen, such as Olaman, Spry and Billy Brass, long-established Murton dealers. Mam did most of her shopping at the Store, but she also gave an order to Billy Brass. Billy was a rough-mannered man of ruddy complexion, the possessor of an ear-splitting voice that perfectly complemented his massively rotund frame. He reputedly had a prodigious appetite for Guinness. A flat cloth cap was always perched on his head, usually at an angle, so that the peak stuck out at the side. He sat sideways on the limbers, the reins hanging loose in his hands, his short legs dangling between the horse's rear and the front wheel of the cart.

How milk was delvered in the 1930s and '40s – by horse and cart.

When I was small, I would accompany Mam out to the cart, but holding back, sheltering behind her, for Billy could be intimidating to a small boy. If he had a queue of customers waiting to be served, he might put the feedbag on the horse, which would then happily munch away on its ration of oats.

As he weighed and bagged the produce, Billy kept up a running monologue. 'That's sprouts, potatoes – any onions? No? I've got some nice tomatoes today, Mrs – here, feel that.' And he would hand one to my mother for inspection. 'Nice and firm, eh. Two pound alright? Right you are, two pound it is, Mrs. Anything else?' Mam would cast her eyes over the cart, and if he had pea pods, she might buy me a bag. My eyes would light up at that,

When Billy had filled my mother's order and given her her change from the moneybag hanging from his shoulder, he would incline his head in my direction and ask needlessly, 'Does he like nuts, then?'

Mam, as a young woman.

Then Mam would hold out her apron and Billy would fill it with monkey nuts from his pan. His customers seen to, Billy would hoist himself back on to the cart, and with a flick of the reins would be off, his voice ringing out in advertisement of his presence in a curious, faintly melodic, jumble of words: 'Ripetomataysweecookinappulll!'

Motor cars were so rarely seen in Murton as to be virtually non-existent. Mr and Mrs Richardson, who lived next door up to us, had a married daughter, Ida, whose husband owned one.

The Richardsons were friendly with my parents, and one day, amidst a general air of excitement, we were invited to go for a drive in their son-in-law's car. Mam and I settled comfortably in the rear seats, marvelling at the leather upholstery and chrome door handles, which seemed to us the height of luxury, while Dad sat in the front with Ida's husband. Off we went with the engine purring, up the front street as far as the Council Schools at the end, before turning right, where we headed in the direction of Cornwall. Mam sat regally at one window, and I gazed intently out of the other. Places we had seen a thousand times before flashed past us in quick succession, giving us a new perspective on them. People stopped to peer curiously as we drove by, and I remember waving to someone I knew.

We covered perhaps a mile and a half in a roughly circular direction, taking in much of Murton, before coming to a stop where the journey had begun, at the front gate. I clambered out of the car with some reluctance. It would still be many years before I sat in another one.

The coal bunker that delivered concessionary coals was one of the few motorized vehicles regularly seen on the streets. It was a tipper, with four compartments, each containing a 15 cwt load of coal. The loads were dropped in the street by the coal hatch.

Like others of my age, I habitually endangered life and limb obtaining a ride by hanging on to the tailgate of the coal bunker once it was in motion. If the driver noticed, he would stop the vehicle and we would run away, but at other times, he might bide his time before deliberately coming to a stop over a large puddle, so when we dropped off we would get our boots and socks wet.

Most houses had a coalhouse at the bottom of the yard, with a hatch facing the street. The hatch was secured on the inside with either a bolt or a sneck, but was opened once the load had arrived to allow the coals

HOW ARE YOU OFF FOR COALS?

A well-known advert for coal.

Young 'uns putting the coal in.

to be thrown in. The open doorway of the coalhouse would be built up of off-cuts of tongue and groove timber up to a height of four or five feet, to avoid coals spilling into the yard when the coalhouse door was opened. If the road surface was concreted, then shovelling coals off it was relatively easy. However, the back of Coronation Street West was then a dirt road, and very uneven. When it rained, rivulets of water meandered down the street, creating a shallow trench in the middle. Shovelling coals off this surface was no easy matter.

Every load of coal contained roundies, big chunks of coal, which were useful for propping up the timbers in the doorway of the coalhouse, and a thick coal dust called duff. Too much duff, and you might hear the recipient complaining, 'Have you seen the load 'ee's brought? Nowt but bloody muck!' When the coals had been put in and the ground swept clean, the duff would be left in a neat pile against the wall.

Not every household had someone who worked at the pit, and those that didn't would have the expense of buying their coal. So it was not unusual, once the load had been put in, to have someone calling at the door asking diplomatically, 'Do you want your duff?' The duff would then be taken away in a wheelbarrow or in pails, to be mixed with their own supply of bought coals, so they would last longer.

Some men, like Dad, put their own coals in. Others preferred to pay the going rate and have someone else do the job. Schoolboys of adequate age and physique, eager to earn a shilling or two, would knock politely on the door before asking, 'Can Aa put your coals in, Mrs?' In my last year at school, I went home for lunch; so did Bobby Kerrison, a friend and classmate. Bobby and I regularly stopped off on the way home to put a load of coal in, earning a shilling each to augment our pocket money. We got so good at it we could do the job in under fifteen minutes, be home for lunch and a quick wash and back at school before afternoon lessons began.

The obligation to work shifts meant that there were always men sleeping during the daylight hours, so the coal motor and the horse-drawn carts constituted noisy distractions. Children too, in their excitable way, could raise the noise level of the street considerably. When it got too strident, inevitably some irate housewife would appear at the door demanding, 'Can you lot make less noise, there's a man in tub-loadin' tryin to get some sleep!' After a mumbled apology, the offenders would move off to play elsewhere.

Other clamorous, and colourful, visitors to the street added to the problem, as the world outside echoed to a cacophony of sounds of a kind unknown today. Occasionally, the collar herring vendor appeared, trumpeting 'Colla' Herrin'!' in his high-pitched nasal voice, as he led his little horse and cart piled with boxes of herring up and down the back streets. A terse cry of 'Any Rags?' would prompt a quick search for the bundles of old clothing awaiting the arrival of the rag-and-bone man. Minor industries of an itinerant genre made fleeting appearances. The unmistakeable rasping sound of metal on stone indicated the presence of the scissors grinder. The scissors grinder provided a useful service for housewives, and an entertainment of sorts for the children of the street, who looked on at a safe distance as he sharpened a variety of implements amidst a shower of sparks, operating the foot pedal to maintain the momentum of the grindstone. When important news warranted it, a messenger from the Colliery Office would appear in the street, the loud staccato of his whirling crake preceding the announcement made at the top of his lungs: 'Meetin' in the Miners' Hall at two o'clock ...' Scenes such as these now seem quaint, even within the memory of those who recall them. At the time, they were part and parcel of the ongoing life of a vibrant community, and the unfortunate sleeper had to develop an immunity to their occurrence.

Drinking men were well provided for in the number of pubs and clubs operating in Murton. Durham pitmen had a habit of bestowing nicknames on their drinking establishments, so that often the legitimate name was all but forgotten. In Murton parlance, the Victoria Inn was always alluded to as the High House, the Victoria Club as the Big Club, the Democratic Club as the Demi Club, the Traveller's Rest as the Back o' the Shaft, and the Colliery Inn, perversely, as the Colliery Inn.

Men and boys gathered outside the Colliery Inn.

The High House was also known as the Irishmen's pub, or the Pat and Micks, because frequented by many Catholic men. To those who were not of this persuasion, the words Catholic and Irish were synonymous. Indeed, in the rare manifestation of an old but waning prejudice, the Pope could still sometimes be referred to, uncharitably and inaccurately, as 'that Irish bugger in the Vatican.'

The Salvation Army sometimes conducted services on a corner between the Colliery Inn and the Traveller's Rest, which, for the purpose of netting sinners, was an appropriately well-chosen pitch. Hardened drinkers vacating these premises, and feeling uplifted by the rousing strains of the Army band, had been known to swear off the drink and pledge themselves to perpetual sobriety. More usually it was a conversion of short duration, when in the cold light of the following day the newfound religious fervour had cooled and the stark implications of a life of teetotalism had sunk in.

The Big Club had an outbuilding with a flat roof. Once the drainpipe had been scaled – an easy matter for a young boy – the roof afforded a view through a window directly into the concert room of the club. From here, I and my fellow delinquents would spy on the grown-ups inside, and perhaps indulge a fancied appetite by proxy, until we were discovered and chased from the scene by one or other of the committee men. We consoled ourselves with the thought that there would come a day when legitimate access to such, erstwhile forbidden, pleasures would be ours.

Knaresboro Road, Murton. 9166.

Another of Murton's pubs – The Knaresboro Hotel.

My friends in the street were mostly older than me, so in more ways than one I looked up to the likes of Ivan Stobie, Jimmy Grieveson and Madeline Burrel, and was content to follow where they led. Doris Hardy, who lived next door, was about a year older than me, and I admired her for being pretty and because she could climb trees better than me.

Peter Flynn lived lower down the street; his father was an official at the pit and his mother was a schoolteacher; he and I had many set-tos, arguing, as boys do, about nothing of any consequence. Peter's favourite actor was Pat O'Brien, while mine was James Cagney. Both actors were renowned for projecting a tough guy image, and we would argue about who was the toughest. Oddly enough, Pat O'Brien was also noted for portraying priests. I don't know if this influenced Peter in any way, but when he grew up he joined the Jesuits and won the prestigious Stanhope History Prize at Oxford.

Two streets away in Windsor Terrace lived Cliffy Nichols, my oldest friend. I first made Cliffy's acquaintance when we moved into Coronation Street shortly before the war, when I was little more than a toddler. Windsor Terrace was concreted, and suitable for ball games and games such as statues and scissors and whipping tops, so I played here a lot, often calling on Cliffy. This was true in the literal sense. To call on a friend you never knocked on the door, but customarily stood there while repeatedly calling the friend's name until the friend came out or until his mother appeared to say he wasn't coming out.

Billy Sparrow, the blacksmith's son, lived in the bottom house in the street. Billy had an olly-gig that had been made at the forge and which he let me borrow. An olly-gig had two parts, an iron hoop and an iron rod with a hook at one end that was used to propel the hoop along the ground. The hoop would go as fast as the person guiding it could run. When used skilfully, it could be made to turn corners and stop abruptly. By pressing down on the hoop with the hook and following through in a forward motion, the hoop could be made to go forward, stop, and reverse, an action embodying a principle well-known to snooker players.

The carts that delivered to the door did not fulfil all our requirements, and Mam routinely put on her hat and coat and went, shopping basket in hand, to the Store or to Fletchers the butchers, where we bought our meat. She didn't always go alone; her sister, Vera called at our house at least once a week, on her way to the shops. Aunty Vera was six years younger than Mam, dark and slight of build just like Mam, but wholly dissimilar in temperament. Though very far from being a humourless person, Mam was nevertheless disposed to be serious-minded, even, on occasion, strait-laced. Vera was ingenuous and carefree; she chewed gum, a habit that Mam rather frowned on as being unladylike, and

A group of Durham lads – the boy at the front is holding a hoop.

she liked to take me to Sunderland to see Shirley Temple pictures. Sometimes Vera came to our house accompanied by my grandmother, and the three women would sit and talk about the latest Utility wear the Store had on offer, or what they planned to do with the divi when it was due. But if ever we ran short of something Mam needed in a hurry and she was too busy to go the shops herself, she would send me.

About the time Cornwall was being built, construction began on a single street of shops only yards from the pit, which, when completed, extended, from top to bottom, about four hundred yards. The street became not only the focus of the commercial life of the colliery, but also the nerve centre of its social life, a forum for discussion, where news was exchanged and gossip disseminated, and, at weekends, after the cinemas closed, a favourite meeting place for the young. Officially, it was named Woods Terrace, but to Murton folk it only ever was referred to as the 'Terrace'.

The 'Terrace' – the centre for commercial and social life in Murton.

The Store was located in the middle of the Terrace and had an entrance back and front, making it possible to take a short cut to the shops through the back door, exiting via the food department at the front. The food department was always busy; and fairly noisy, as the wooden balls of the cash retrieval system were constantly being propelled onto the overhead track, which took them from the various serving counters to the cashier's office and then back again. A distinctive aroma greeted the nostrils immediately on entering, a pleasant, mixed aroma of dairy produce, spices and cold meats, for, of course, nothing came pre-packed. Bacon and ham were sliced into the desired thickness on the bacon slicer, before being weighed and served.

An early view of the staff of the Murton Co-operative Society.

Butter and cheese came in great blocks, so had to be cut into the required size and approximate weight with an instrument consisting of a length of wire with a wooden handle at each end. Bread was sold uncut, and biscuits sold loose from tins. All general stores sold food in this way. General stores doing business on the Terrace that could count their employees on the fingers of more than one hand were Skilbecks, Walter Willsons, the Meadow Dairy and Thompson's Red Stamp Stores, which came nearest to matching the Co-operative Store both in the number of its employees and of its customers.

Walter Willson's – one of the many stores on the 'Terrace.'

In addition to these food emporiums, the Terrace boasted a post office, a police station, two medical practices, a chemist's shop and a dentist. The highest building on the Terrace was the white, marble-faced tower of the Store Clock, Murton's version of Big Ben. The chimes could be heard all over Murton when it struck the hour; but that only happened when it was in working order, which wasn't that often. Two of Murton's oldest and busiest pubs, the Colliery Inn and the Traveller's Rest, traded at the foot of the Terrace. I'm sure it was purely fortuitous, and of no intended symbolic significance, that looking down on them from the top end were the Temperance Institute and a Methodist chapel.

Within this microcosmic economy flourished numerous small businesses. Meat could be bought at any one of half-a-dozen butchers shops, and fish at Moore's wet fish shop, if desired fresh; but for a quick meal, Hall's and Mary Jane's fish and chip shops were both close by. Stobie's sold tobacco and confectionary, Pioli's ice creams and hot and cold drinks, and Bucknalls the baker's cakes and pies were unrivalled anywhere. You went to Walker's for household electrical goods and Harland's for draperies; and if your boots or shoes were in need of repair, there was Arnold Johnson's cobblers shop across the road in nearby Durham Place. A thriving commerce took place here, within the shadow of the pit. And it was the pit that sustained it: directly or indirectly, the pit furnished the means by which an entire population satisfied its material needs; and, to further broaden its ambit, it generated the social milieu wherein all other needs were met.

WOODS TERRACE, MURTON COLLIERY. 1630.

Looking down Woods Terrace with the Officials' Club on the left.

SECTION TWO

BEGINNING SCHOOL

Murton young 'uns enjoying themselves at school in 1950.

On high ground, about a mile to the west of the colliery, lies the old village of Murton, at the time the pit was sunk a hamlet of not more than a half-dozen houses. Over the years, with the mushrooming of council housing estates, the distance between colliery and village gradually diminished, until eventually the westward expansion absorbed the village completely.

In the 1870s, the parish church of Holy Trinity was erected mid-way between the colliery and the village. Much later, the Catholic church of St Joseph's appeared about a hundred yards below its Anglican counterpart on what became known as the church bank. Facing the church on the other side of a busy road, and pre-dating it by about thirty years, was St Joseph's Catholic School. The school was older and smaller than the impressive-looking Council School, which could be seen for miles around from its lofty position on the crest of a rise five hundred yards west of the pit.

St Joseph's could accommodate about two hundred and fifty pupils. Most of the classrooms were situated on one side of the building, separated by folding partition walls of wood frame and glass. The partitions could be slid to one side to create a hall of notable size suitable for social functions, and since the school existed before St Joseph's parish acquired its first church, for many years it served as a chapel for Sunday services.

On passing out of the school gates at the end of the school day, pupils either turned right and made their way towards the colliery houses of Cornwall, or turned left and headed up the church bank in the direction of the newer, and what were thought to be more posh, council houses. In either case, most pupils had best part of a mile to walk before arriving home.

Children in the yard of the Council School.

St Joseph's School.

In common with every pupil who passed through St Joseph's School, I was taught almost exclusively by women teachers. In this regard, we differed from the boys of the Council School, whose experience was generally the opposite. The headmistress, Miss Riley, was a middle-aged, rather severe figure, who did hardly any teaching but was an administrator, and occupied an office at one end of the corridor. Almost the only contact I had with Miss Riley was when I got into trouble and was sent to her office to be caned. There were six assistant teachers, one to each class, and all subjects were taught by the class teacher.

The considerable Irish influx into the Durham coalfield over the years was reflected in the number of pupils bearing Irish names, and since the teachers were for the most part of identical ethnic origin, most of those also had Irish names. Two were Irish. The sisters, Mary and Annie Gallagher were by any standard formidable women. Mary, the elder of the two, was six feet tall, with straight black hair and a rich voice with a hint of a brogue. She taught the senior pupils of the top class, and though always respectfully addressed to her face as Miss Gallagher, was known to parents and pupils alike as Big Gal. Annie also was big, and, like her sister, unmarried, though in later life she did marry. She taught the reception class, or babies, and partly for this reason and partly to distinguish her from her, marginally bigger, sister, was incongruously dubbed Little Gal. Fear had a conspicuous place in the teaching method of both sisters, as those who misbehaved or displayed a stubborn reluctance to learn were to discover. Little Gal was much given to outbursts of temper, and at such times could be heard in all parts of the school. Sardonic wit was a particular attribute of Big Gal, who was noted for her devastating put-downs. It was impressed upon every pupil that the 'g' in the middle of Gallagher was silent, and anyone slow to heed this important lesson in pronunciation and omit the sound of the redundant letter would be verbally flayed alive.

In order of ascendance, infants to seniors, the remaining teachers were Miss Daly, Miss Madigan, Miss McGann and Miss Gibson. The unmarried state was not a qualification for employment at the school; nevertheless it was never my experience to be taught by a married teacher.

For my first day at school, I left the house well-scrubbed and fitted-out in a neat new outfit of matching jacket and short trousers, shoes and stockings and, it being wartime, with the indispensable accoutrement of a Mickey Mouse gas mask slung over my shoulder. Fresh-faced and not unduly apprehensive, I braved the unknown, conscious of the fact that I was embarking upon a new and important stage in the process of growing up. I would be joining

Dad relaxing on holiday.

my seniors, older children like Cliffy and Peter Flynn, who already went to the school. Shortly before, one of my walks with Dad had taken us to the top of the church bank at a time when school was out and the playing field behind the school teeming with noisy young revellers. From our vantage point opposite, everybody seemed to be having great fun, running wild and tumbling about on the grass, yelling excitedly. 'That's school,' Dad murmured laconically, and indicated that very soon I would be joining the revellers. He meant to be reassuring, but this might just have given me a one-sided impression of what lay in store for me as a scholar.

It was entirely typical that my first morning of school life was the only time I was taken to school by my mother, and that at lunch time and again at the end of the school day, I found my own way home. Unaccustomed to being abruptly removed from the secure surroundings of home and left in the care of strangers, many children broke down and cried once their mothers had departed. Some ran home at the first opportunity and had to be brought back. I was unprepared for the shock when it dawned on me that Mam would no longer always be there, and that henceforth I would have to get used to this strange new environment of classrooms and authority figures and regimentation. Determined that I was not going to cry, much as I wanted to, I somehow managed to hold back the tears. In time, everyone got over their homesickness and settled into the routine of regular school attendance.

The babies was a bright classroom, with tall, many-paned windows on two sides that faced the outside; consequently, it enjoyed the sun for best part of the day. It was also a warm room; in addition to the central heating pipes running along the bottom of the walls, it was the only classroom to have an open fire. This was situated directly behind Little Gal's desk and was always surrounded by a heavy, square fireguard. The fireguard was regularly used to dry tea towels, and, in inclement weather, the gloves and hats of pupils who had been caught in the wet. There was a plentiful supply of fuel, so the fire always glowed cheerily, and the nearness of desk to fire must have resulted in Little Gal always having a well-warmed posterior.

We sat at small desks on moveable chairs, around the back of which was hung our coats and gas masks; desks and chairs were arranged in four sections and seating arrangements went according to age. A wheeled blackboard in a massive wood and metal frame stood at the front of the classroom; whenever it had to be moved, it squeaked loudly and made the floor shake. Hanging from the wall to the side of the fireplace was a large picture in a gilt frame of a little girl in Edwardian costume, dwarfed by an old English sheepdog, the educational significance of which escaped me but which was comforting to gaze at.

We played with beads a lot, used crayons for colouring our own pictures, and made figures with plasticine of different colours. When it came to serious learning, I copied my letters and did my sums with chalk, writing on a slate with a wooden frame.

Miss Daly played the piano for morning assembly, when everyone, pupils and teachers, crammed together in the narrow corridor with the cracked, concrete floor, and the school day began with prayers and hymn-singing. The school had two pianos: the newer one was kept permanently in Miss Gibson's classroom, and was used for music lessons; but every morning an old broken-down piano was wheeled out of Miss Madigan's classroom and into the corridor, and then wheeled back again at the conclusion of assembly.

As a general rule, the choice of hymns was dictated by the liturgical year. Approaching Pentecost, we accordingly raised our voices to *Come Holy Ghost, Creator Come*. In Our Lady's months of May and October, the school echoed to the strains of *I'll Sing a Hymn to Mary* and *Bring Flowers of the Rarest, bring Blossoms the Fairest*. At Christmastime, we had an enormous repertoire of hymns that included not only perennial favourites known to everyone like *Angels we have heard on High*, *Adeste Fideles* among many others, but also lesser-known Christmas hymns such as *Sleep Holy Babe*, which, sadly, seem to have fallen out of favour and are rarely heard any more.

The degree of enthusiasm for the singing depended on the prevailing mood – Monday usually was a poor day – or on the popularity of the hymn. If the singing showed signs of flagging, the headmistress, Miss Riley would call a halt to it. The piano would fall silent, heads would go down, there would be some embarrassed shuffling of feet, and in a voice that was firm but never raised above normal pitch, Miss Riley would berate us for our lack of effort. 'Dear oh dear, that was dreadful, simply dreadful. Surely you can do better than that. They can sing louder than that, Miss Gallagher.'

'I'm sure they can, Miss Riley,' Big Gal would concur.

Pausing pointedly, Miss Riley would fix the assembled choristers with a stare that was felt by everyone to be directed exclusively at themselves. 'Shall we try that again, then; and for goodness sake put more life into it this time. From the second verse, Miss Daly …'

As the notes from the battered old piano rang out, Big Gal would be heard exhorting the top class to greater efforts. 'Sing the lot of you. Let me catch anyone not singing …'

There was no need to complete the threat. Heads everywhere would go back, lungs would expand, and this time everybody would sing to raise the roof.

My first few weeks at school proved to me one thing: that the irresistible attraction that draws one towards members of the opposite sex begins to be felt at a very tender age. Elizabeth Hagen was a five-year-old beauty with dark, wavy hair that reached to her waist. Her family had come from Jarrow on Tyneside. Jarrow was then a byword for economic depression, but to me it was another name for heaven. If Elizabeth Hagen had come from there, then I knew it had to be a place where the sun shone all the time and happiness reigned. It was only an abrupt change in family circumstances that had brought about her temporary exile from heaven. Somehow it didn't seem right that such a creature should remain long in a mundane place like Murton, and Elizabeth was a pupil at St Joseph's School only a short time before her parents transported her back to the earthly paradise of Jarrow-upon-Tyne.

Norman Burns was the first new friend I made, and we remained friends throughout school, sharing a fondness for books and later, when we were both in the top class, playing on the same football team. Cliffy Nichols, who I regularly associated with in the street, had been going to school about eighteen months when I started and so was in a higher class than me, but I occasionally caught a glimpse of him in the corridor at assembly, and at playtime, when I spied him through the railings separating the boys playground from the girls, where I, as a new starter, was at first confined.

Dullards and idlers were anathema to Little Gal, and even those who worked assiduously and never put a foot wrong could find her unnerving. Among my contemporaries in her class were the twins Colin and Clive Burke. They must have been fraternal twins for they didn't look much alike; Colin had sandy-coloured hair and was of slight build, whereas Clive was dark and the bigger of the two. They were townies, that is, they originated from Sunderland; after only a few years living in Murton, the family returned to Sunderland and I never saw them again. Colin and Clive were cheerful, devil-may-care types who appeared to have been successfully inoculated against learning. No matter how much Little Gal raged at them, they remained resolutely uninstructed and unbowed. Their unremitting cheerfulness and complete indifference to punishment were a constant provocation to Little Gal, so that they became the principal objects of her wrath. Since

Little Gal in one of her rages was terrible to behold, I thanked my lucky stars for that happy combination of coincidental events – conception, birth, proximity of abode, and religion – that had established Colin and Clive in the same class as me.

An eagerly-awaited break from lessons came at playtime, when we took full advantage of our temporary freedom to let off steam outside, and when staff members could shed their classroom image for a while and retire to Miss Riley's office for tea and biscuits and a few moments of convivial fellowship.

All classrooms opened on to the corridor, from where, at playtime and hometime, the boys exited at one end and the girls at the other; new starters, however, entered and left by a door at the back of Little Gal's classroom, which opened on to a flight of steps leading down to the girls' play area. At first, both girls and boys played here. Later, the boys gained access to the boys' yard, and to the playing field behind the school, where on its green, undulating surface fun fights and ball games, and games of Cowboys and Indians took place.

Prominently situated on the edge of the playing field, was a row of brick and concrete bomb shelters, one for every class. They were covered in turf and, at playtime, became a sort of adventure playground. Fun fights took place on their sloping sides, while races were held from the top to the bottom of the field with the shelters as obstacles. Rarely, if at all, were the shelters used for the purpose for which they were intended, for air raids invariably took place at night. At the corner of each shelter, a short flight of concrete steps led down to the heavy, steel door. The doors had once been painted red, but the paint had flaked on all of them and now they were edged with rust. To open and close the door, it was necessary to turn a large wheel, which was always stiff and difficult to operate. Once inside, with the door shut tight, the shelter was as black as a tomb. Claustrophobics had to be on

Annie Gallagher, 'Little Gal', with a first communion class.

their guard, as playtimes could be hazardous. Entombing younger boys was an amusing diversion for the more sadistically-inclined bigger lads, most especially Arnie Gruthious, who was then in the upper juniors but built like a senior. So Arnie, and one or two like him, had to be quickly recognised and thereafter avoided

Late in the afternoon, when everything had been cleared away and the milk monitor had been to remove the crate of empties, the story book would come out, and Little Gal would read to us the tales of Brer Rabbit and Brer Fox. This was the best part of the day, when the teacher was in a mellow mood, and when every pupil, even the normally uncooperative ones like Colin and Clive, was quiet and attentive, and young minds were receptive to the magic of story time.

Once I was promoted to the top section, I came under the direct gaze of Little Gal, whose desk was at the head of the section. At this stage, I had outgrown slate and chalk and was writing with a pencil in an exercise book. If a mistake was made, you had to go to the teacher's desk to ask for a rubber. If you went too often, she grumbled, so you were tempted to use your finger to rub out your mistakes; this left a black mark on the page and landed you in further trouble. We read from readers that were graded according to the colours green, blue and red. Despite her volatile temperament, Little Gal must have been a good teacher, for by the time I left the babies I had gone through all three books of the colour scheme.

Miss Daly's classroom faced Little Gal's across the corridor; it was rather a drab room, for the only windows to face outside were high up in the wall. The walls of Miss Daly's classroom were hung with coloured charts, and pictures depicting the seasons of the year, and this went some way towards brightening up the room. We sat on benches with tip-up seats and solid iron frames, and the desks had raised tops, inside which we kept our school books.

Miss Daly was young and bespectacled and smelled of red ink. Unlike Little Gal, she rarely raised her voice. We were taught short division and the multiplication tables, which we learnt by rote, reciting them aloud in unison in sing-song voices. I learnt how to write with pen and ink, being careful not to blot my work or get the pen nib crossed so that it would no longer write and had to be changed. The ink well was set into a round hole in the corner of the desk, and could be removed to be re-filled or washed. Ink monitors periodically topped them up from stone jars.

My first day at school now seemed a long way behind me, and the current crop of new starters who sat apprehensively at their desks in Little Gal's classroom appeared very much younger than me. Just as I had looked up to Cliffy and Peter, now I was one of the older ones that others looked up to. Nevertheless, I did have one regret about moving up a class, which belied my growing sense of maturity. Being no longer one of the babies meant that I was obliged to hand in my Mickey Mouse gas mask in exchange for the conventional type; this I did with the greatest reluctance and a keen sense of loss.

VISITING RELATIVES

Mam, Granda, Uncle Joe, Grandma and Vera outside Fatten Pasture back door.

Little white coffins were hardly ever seen in my day, but in my parents time they were a familiar sight.

Dad came from a family of eleven children, but there was never a time when there were eleven children living, and only four of the eleven attained to adulthood. Of five boys, Dad was the only one to survive infancy. Three of Dad's sisters also died young. So the family as I knew it consisted of Dad and his three surviving sisters, two older and one younger than himself.

My paternal grandmother departed this life early in 1922, just days short of her fiftieth birthday, and, though a non-Catholic, was the first person to be buried in the Catholic churchyard. She was followed into her grave two years later by my grandfather, who was fifty-two when he died. My grandmother died as a result of catching a chill while wallpapering someone's house. She and my grandfather were at one time caretakers of St Joseph's School, and my grandfather also worked at the pit.

Aunt Ellen was ten years older than Dad and the eldest in the family. She and Uncle Jim Morris had a council house on a large estate that had sprouted up in the decade before the war. Aunt Jennie, who was two years younger than Aunt Ellen, lived around the corner on the same estate with her husband, Jimmy Green. It was an odd circumstance that all three of Dad's sisters married men with the same Christian name as himself.

Aunt Ellen was like my mother in one respect: neither were very good visitors. When my cousin, Mary, had one of her birthday parties I was always invited, and always pleased to attend, even though she was some years older than me, otherwise I was myself an infrequent visitor to the house. As a partial excuse, I can

Dad's parents – the grandparents I never knew.

plead at least one mitigating circumstance: Aunt Ellen was a workhorse, and to catch her at an idle moment was well-nigh impossible. Her working week was arranged according to an unvarying routine which she religiously adhered to. If she wasn't grafting her way through a mountain of ironing when I called, she would be furiously possing the weekly wash, sleeves rolled up to her elbows, or engaged in some other menial but necessary occupation, for which she seemed endowed by nature with a special propensity.

Aunt Ellen was conscientious, forthright, sharp and argumentative when she perceived a wrong, but kindly. She was always pleased to see me on the odd occasions when I called at the house, and would stop whatever she was doing long enough to sit and chat.

Aunt Ellen and Uncle Jim Morris.

Sometimes we would have to sit beneath an arrangement of damp clothes strung out to dry on lines which criss-crossed the living room. She sat upright on a straight-back chair – nothing would have induced her to leave her work and relax in an armchair – and since I was always conscious of a vague notion that every minute of her day was accounted for, I was careful not to overstay my welcome.

Aunt Elsie, Dad's youngest sister, was well-educated; the fact that she had been to college and qualified as a schoolteacher was a matter of family pride. She and her husband, Jimmy Eyre, and their four children lived three miles away at New Seaham, called by locals the Nack, for reasons unknown, though theories abound. Of my four Eyre cousins, Jimmy was nearest my own age, and we were very friendly for a time. Joan, the eldest, was five years older than me and had been a bridesmaid at my parents wedding. I thought her very grown-up, and was flattered when she attended my seventh birthday party with the rest of my cousins. While they were living at the Nack, Uncle Jimmy was involved in a Catholic organization known as the Knights of St Columba. Every Christmastime, the Knights gave a party for the local children and he always saw to it that I received a ticket, even though, living out of the area, I wasn't strictly entitled to one. The highlight of the evening occurred at the end when, as they were leaving, each child was given a box of cream cakes to take home.

Later, the family moved to Billingham on Teesside; after that, contact between us was sporadic. Dad once took me to someone's birthday party at Billingham and it took three buses to get there, if you included the bus from Murton across to the Waterworks. It was late when we got back to Murton, but I enjoyed myself so much it made the journey worthwhile. The event has acquired a nostalgic piquancy, becoming one of those landmarks in memory that we all have and take pleasure in recalling, even though the particulars in this case remain hazy.

After a short interval, the Eyres moved on again, this time to Slough in Buckinghamshire, and I regret to say we saw even less of one another subsequently, when it was always they who returned north to see us.

As my maternal grandparents, Grandma and Granda Slater, were the only grandparents I knew, I saw rather a lot of them. They had their home on the outskirts of Murton, a little over a mile from where we lived. To get there, you had to cross the Terrace and then follow a road that skirted the pithead and the end houses of Cornwall opposite.

Formally, the pithead was more or less open, but in the 1920s a high surrounding wall was built which partly shut it off from public view. The enclosure of the pithead gave rise to a mixed sense of curiosity and foreboding in those, especially children such as myself, who had never ventured beyond the enclosing wall.

MURTON COLLIERY. 1639.

Murton Colliery from the south west.

As pit villages go, Murton was not altogether lacking in charm. The surrounding farmland, the hilly terrain over which straggled its rows of snug houses, the fact that it grew up alongside a rural village of medieval foundation which it eventually absorbed, all were factors which served to mitigate the impression of industrial ugliness often associated with pit villages. Regardless of all that, the pit undeniably dominated the village, signifying its massive physical presence in various ways. Its sights and sounds and the sulphuric smell which hung about the air within its immediate vicinity were to most people familiar experiences, especially to me, as I was a regular caller at my grandparents house, and any route other than past the pithead would have more than doubled the distance. It was a noisy place. Day and night could be heard the low rumble of tubs on the move, followed by the abrupt crash of the buffers impacting, and the metallic clash of the coupling chain as it swung to and fro, lashing the wheels of the tubs. Hissing jets of steam seemed always to be escaping from some structure or other, mingling with the smoke from the pit chimney, before vanishing into the atmosphere. High above, loomed the colliery winding gear, which periodically creaked into motion, like the awakening of some prehistoric beast from an indeterminate sleep. Quickly gaining speed until its double wheels were spinning silently, it brought coals to bank, and, at the end of the shift, men.

The pit wall was rendered all round; the longest stretch, that facing Cornwall, extended for roughly four hundred yards, and was broken only by the pit gates midway across. Through these gates at various times of day passed silent, white-faced men bound for work. Other, more jovial, men, their shift completed, came out homeward bound. Once they would have been covered with the primeval grime of the pit, but following the opening of the Pithead Baths in 1939, men no longer walked home from work black,

Pithead baths – a luxury to the pitman of the 1930s.

and the practice of washing down in the tin bath by the fire was preserved in memory as a faintly droll anachronism. Once past the end of the pit wall, there was still about a third of a mile to go to my grandparents' house; most of this distance was covered by allotments, a haphazard assemblage of wooden crees, chicken wire, old doors and miscellaneous bits of fencing.

Grandma and Granda, and Uncle Joe, my mother's older brother, lived in an old, crooked dwelling that had once been a tied farm cottage. There were two such dwellings in addition to the main farmhouse; the other cottage housed a family of the name of Brown. Farmhouse and cottages and the surrounding land bore the collective and rustic-sounding name of Fatten Pasture. The buildings have all long since gone, and the land is now under cultivation. It is possible that the properties were at that time in the possession of the coal owners, for my grandparents lived rent-free, which was the reason they chose to live there when they could have lived more commodiously in a council house. My grandfather was a surface worker, and poorly paid in comparison with underground workers.

Like the houses of Cornwall, which it overlooked from its slightly higher elevation, Fatten Pasture was a brick-built bungalow with a slate roof and old fashioned sash windows. A water barrel stood at the back door to collect the rain water, and a tin bath hung from the wall at the side, for, like most houses at the time, including our own, the cottage lacked a bathroom. The low-ceiling interior consisted on one level of a living room and two bedrooms. Come down a step from the living room, and you would be standing on the stone flags of the kitchen, worn glass smooth by generations of labouring folk.

The Slaters and the Browns shared a garden at the back amounting to more than half an acre, and a water tap, the only source of water except for the rain-water barrel, inconveniently sited thirty yards down the garden path. The water tap was an ornamental type, shaped like a lion's head, with a round, fluted handle on one side. The handle being heavy, was not easy for a child to operate, but when turned the water came out of the lion's mouth. A metal shelf about ten inches from the ground took the weight of the water bucket while it was being filled, while the overspill leaked away through a drain at ground level. The two families had separate though adjacent water closets, brick-built and white-washed within, but, like the water tap, some distance removed from the house. Nothing was ever grown out the back except a few flowers beneath the kitchen window, so the grass, and the sheep sorrel and fat hen that mingled with it, grew to three or four feet in places. A stone wall surrounded

Mam and Grandma.

the garden, too high for me to climb, which was just as well for the drop into the field beyond was considerable. In the summer months, the pointed leaf and white, bell-like blossoms of the hedge bindweed sprawled along the wall from end to end in thick profusion. I enjoyed playing out here in the long grass, but would nip smartly into the house whenever Mrs Brown appeared. She never spoke to anyone but was always muttering to herself, and I was afraid of her.

In distinct contrast to the wilderness of the back, the front of the dwelling looked out on to a neat, gravel-covered driveway, which was used by the family occupying the farmhouse opposite. On the narrowest patch of garden, mint grew in profusion up to the window ledge. Apart from flowers, it was the only thing my grandparents grew, and they and my mother had home-grown mint on the dinner table every Sunday. A foot scraper stood to the right of the door, always in immaculate condition, for the only two occasions when anyone entered or left the house by the front door was when my mother and my Aunt Vera were married.

Uncle Joe was two years older than my mother, and a bachelor; the two of them had been inseparable as children and remained very close. Uncle Joe was short and stocky and, like Mam, had dark hair and brown eyes; judging from photographs taken of him when in his youth, he might have been considered handsome. He made a big fuss over me, as I was the first of his nephews and nieces.

Grandma Slater had rosy cheeks and a round face that was completely unlined. Like many elderly women, she was plump; most likely she would have considered dieting unhealthy. Also like many elderly women, and unlike most men, she wore glasses. Her dependence on glasses was possibly a result of the hours spent sewing and darning that she, in common with other women, was obliged to do then, and, in my grandmother's case, of the concentration and industry she devoted to the clippy mats which she made in her spare time.

My grandfather always sat by the front window in a brown leather armchair, where he read his newspaper or contentedly smoked his clay pipe. The pipe gave off an acrid smell that clung to the room, but which I found pleasant and comforting. Periodically, he leaned across to the fireplace and gently knocked his pipe on the hob to clear the tobacco ash. It was the only thing he ever smoked. Most old men smoked clay pipes; they were cheap and easily replaced if broken. Jimmy Rankin, the local barber, always kept a supply of them and gave them away to his customers.

Granda Slater was a small, slight man, shorter than Dad by at least two inches. He sported a thick moustache, as did many old men; in this fashion, they differed from the men of my father's generation, who were almost without exception clean-shaven. When he went out, he always wore a three-piece suit, with a watch and chain adorning his waistcoat. Some men attached commemorative medals to their watch chains; a silver sixpence decorated his. It had been awarded to my mother as a prize for knowing the answer to something when she was a little girl at school. My grandfather had asked her if she would allow him to replace it with another, and after boring a hole through the centre, had attached it to his watch chain. Granda Slater was a taciturn man at any time, but when the womenfolk of the family came together he was virtually rendered dumb. My mother, grandmother, and Aunt Vera enjoyed, indeed excelled at, banal conversation, which was conducted always in strident tones. Seated on the pouffe or fireside cracket, which was the only seating available to me when company was present, I observed them with childlike fascination as each strained to talk above the other two. At such times, Granda would wink across at me and a mischievous smile would tug at the corner of his mouth.

Before I was of school age, he would put his jacket on and take me over to the nearby allotments to see the hens. Squatting on his hunkers, he would make clucking noises with his tongue in imitation of the sounds they made in an effort to 'tice them over to where we were. When he succeeded, he would point through the wire mesh and make some needless observation such as 'Look! They're comin' over, see,' and then give me breadcrumbs to throw at them.

Granda Slater would sometimes give me money, but he would think up novel ways of giving it. It was as though displays of generosity embarrassed him. He might pretend that he had a surplus, and would ask me, as a favour, to spend a sixpence for him. Once he took me on a stroll through the dene to the neighbouring village of Dalton-le-Dale. The focal point of Dalton-le-Dale is the medieval church of St Andrew's. According to a local legend, when Oliver Cromwell's men were going around despoiling the churches they passed St Andrew's by because

A postcard view of the picturesque village of Dalton-le-Dale.

The playground at Dalton-le-Dale.

they failed to notice it for the surrounding trees. Thus it remains today, still hidden from view whenever the trees are in leaf.

Two hundred yards past the church, the stream which runs through the village is spanned by an 18th century stone bridge, and from here a rough track climbs above and away from the village. Money Lane, Granda Slater called it, because, as he said, if you looked hard enough and were lucky enough sometimes you could find money lying on the ground. So I strained my eyes, walking bent double, and sure enough every few yards, lying among the dust and the stones, was a threepenny piece. Several times I got lucky, each time excitedly communicating my find to my grandfather, who was walking up ahead, and must have been secretly dropping the coins from his pocket. By the time we arrived back at Fatten Pasture, I had five or six coins, which represented more than a shilling, and was probably more than he could afford to give.

Grandma Slater had been born and raised in the Millfield area of Sunderland, where many of her relatives still lived. Every so often she would put on her black coat and black hat, take her black handbag and go and visit them, taking me with her, when we would walk to the Terrace to take our places at the Store Clock bus stop. The sea was visible on the right-hand side for much of the time, while before us the barrage balloons suspended above the town skyline signposted the way. At Ryhope, about midway, we passed the German POW camp, where the prisoners were ordinarily to be seen at work in the fields. It was a hectic time visiting the various dwellings in the various parts of Millfield, for Grandma's family was scattered. Fatigue set in by the end of the day, making us both doze off on the drive home, and we would usually not awaken until the bus pulled on to the Murton road at the Waterworks. Alighting at the Store Clock, we then had to trudge the three-quarters of a mile past the pithead and the allotments to Fatten Pasture. Once inside the house, Grandma would sink into an armchair with a grateful sigh and observe wistfully that she could do with a cup of tea.

Granda Slater with his sister, Great Aunt Kate.

THE WAR

The war wasn't all doom and gloom as there were plenty of lighter moments as well. Here the Salvation Army are keeping spirits up with a Black and White Minstrel Show in 1940. Mary Ann Taylor (who would not put black on her face) is back row, left.

At the time I was born, the world was moving inexorably towards war; by the time I was ten, it was still coming to terms with the aftermath. It is an awesome thought that the first decade of my existence was dominated by the most apocalyptic series of events in the history of the human race.

Despite being so young, I had some understanding of this. The Second World War was a conflict in every sense universal, such as none before it had been, not even the Great War. But there was everywhere a note of optimism, a conviction that right would prevail; and no one doubted that we were in the right.

Before the outbreak of war, Uncle Joe left his job at the pit, where he had worked since leaving school, and enlisted in the local regiment, the Durham Light Infantry. When war came, he was a member of the British Expeditionary Force, and was picked up unconscious off the beach at Dunkirk with shrapnel wounds, before being returned to England to convalesce. Auntie Vera met her husband, Albert, when both were working at Thompson's Red Stamp Stores on the Terrace. Albert was of good family, and a most agreeable man, who got on well with Mam and Dad. He and Vera were married during the war, and when Albert was home on leave from the RAF, they occupied our spare room upstairs, as they had no home of their own at the time. Uncle Joe and Uncle Albert were both to see service in the Far East.

For those of us living at home, the experience of war was felt in different ways. The war influenced the food we ate, the games we played, even, to some extent, the clothes we wore; and it brought about notable changes in the physical environment with the appearance of

Thompson's Red Stamp Stores, Woods Terrace, in the 1930s.

barrage balloons, pillboxes, bomb shelters, and a water drum at the end of the street big enough and deep enough to swim in.

Rationing and shortages affected everyone. We got used to grey bread, powdered eggs, and government-issue biscuits that looked remarkably like dog biscuits and were almost as hard. Bananas I could remember from before the war, but they, along with my favourite childhood treat, Milky Way, were among the many things that disappeared. Boiled sweets were available, but were rationed, and money was worthless if you lacked coupons. The Ration Book was an accessory to living as familiar then as a cheque book and credit card are today, only it was more essential.

One birthday, I was given two smallish apples as a present, and somehow there would be an apple and an orange in my stocking every Christmas, but I think my parents had to call in a few favours to procure them. Generally, fruit was unobtainable during the war. Adults were probably the most affected by such privations, particularly mothers and fathers of small children; not only having to do without themselves, they suffered the additional hardship of being unable to give their children things once taken for granted.

At the local sweet shop, we could buy something called locust. Locust is mentioned in the Bible, though it should not be confused with the grasshopper-like insect of the same name, which also appears in the Bible, and which also was eaten by humans. Times were hard but we would have drawn the line at eating grasshoppers, no matter that John the Baptist found them palatable.

Locust was also the name of the leguminous fruit of a middle-eastern plant, and we might have had some hesitation in eating it had we known that normally it was fed to cattle. In looks, it resembled over-ripe banana. Once the leathery skin had been prised open, it had a distinctive sweet taste. It wasn't really all that pleasant, and it was only because of the stringency of the times that it found its way into sweetshops at all. In better days, with an abundance of fruit and other things, no one would have touched it.

Every sweet shop sold liquorice root, or cuddy root, as we called it. Cuddy root looked like sticks of wood, but it had a strong, pleasant taste; it was chewed until the last drop of juice had been squeezed out of it, and sometimes long after. Cinnamon sticks could be obtained from chemist shops and were greatly relished for their woody texture and spicy flavour. Some people smoked them, mostly older boys thinking to be adult, and despairing men made strangers to cigarettes.

We discovered that pitch could be chewed like chewing gum. Being harder, it caused the jaws to ache before very long, and the flavour was a poor substitute for Spearmint or Beech Nut. Chewing pitch whitened the teeth, and also produced copious amounts of saliva. Since being able to spit spectacularly in a casual way was a particular affectation of the male adolescent, the saliva would be expelled through the teeth in long streams at every opportunity.

The scarcity of cigarettes was a particular hardship for adults.

Tobacconists receiving a supply of cigarettes would usually ration them, twenty, or perhaps ten, per person. The rumour that 'Stobies have tabs' would spread throughout Murton like a forest fire, and soon a queue of nicotine-craving adults would form outside Cud Stobie's shop to extend maybe fifty yards down the Terrace.

Every smoker kept a machine with which to roll cigarettes, and a supply of cigarette papers. He would also possess a tin, small enough to be carried in the pocket, in which was carried the loose tobacco salvaged from cigarette ends. From the accumulated tobacco, fresh cigarettes could be made. Frugality was thus a universal trait forced on smokers by war-time conditions. Some really desperate types were not above picking up tab ends from the road for the few precious strands of tobacco they contained.

With many shortages during the war the Government produced adverts such as this to help preserve vital supplies.

The war was acted out on the playing fields and in the streets with toy rifles and tommy guns. Imitation weapons, mostly home-made and some not even painted, together with model spitfires and hurricanes, were favourite Christmas presents for boys. Aeroplane glass, spent cartridge cases and, especially, shrapnel were avidly collected and proudly displayed. My jacket pocket bulged with the prized pieces of shrapnel given me by my Uncle Joe. He had spent a long time convalescing after Dunkirk, and, though I didn't realize it at the time, my shrapnel collection had in all probability been extracted from his body.

One day, I arrived home to find a tank parked outside our back door. The neighbourhood kids were swarming all over it. Inside, Uncle Joe was sitting at the kitchen table with a fellow soldier, while my mother was busy feeding them. Uncle Joe looked up when I entered. 'Why, if it isn't Pat, home from school. How've you been, then?' He stopped eating long enough to reach out and ruffle my hair. 'Pat's my nephew,' he explained to his companion.

I felt proud having an uncle in uniform, and faintly envious, thinking, naively, how wonderful it must be to be a soldier and carry a real rifle and travel around in an army tank. Mam was fussing over them, pleased to be of use. 'Do they not feed you in the army, then?' she said jokingly, for the two of them were diving into her home cooking as if they hadn't tasted decent food in days.

Meanwhile, their presence, or more precisely the presence of their tank, was proving a source of great interest outside, where imaginary battles were being fought and cries of 'Jerries comin' over the ridge, Commander!' and 'Fire one round, men,' rang out to the accompaniment of sounds meant to represent exploding shells. Military tanks didn't appear in the street every day, so it was a brief moment of triumph for me. As it was my uncle, I jealously claimed a sort of trusteeship over the tank, insisting that permission be requested before coming aboard; but most of the boys being older than me, my jurisdiction proved to be purely nominal and I was conspicuously ignored. After remaining about an hour, Uncle Joe took his leave of us, and it was shortly after this incident that he was posted to India.

The fears entertained for the safety of those serving in trouble spots abroad could easily make one forgetful of the ever-present dangers lurking nearer home. We were reminded of this fact and cruelly shaken out of any feeling of complacency when in June, 1942 an explosion ripped through the five-quarter seam, killing thirteen men. Murton was not one of those pits that had suffered a major disaster involving great loss of life, but it did have a history of minor disasters. The 1942 explosion, fortunately, was the last of these; for many years subsequently, the average number of fatalities at the pit was never more than two per year.

Uncle Joe in uniform.

In those pre-television days, the wireless was an important means of keeping abreast of developments in the war, and for maintaining morale at home, so it was listened to attentively. Around it we gathered as a family in mutual comfort. Beyond the cosy, well-lit atmosphere inside, was a dark, alien environment, unrelieved by even the faintest chink of light, lest the enemy spot it from the air. Air Raid Wardens patrolled the streets to enforce the regulation, and to ensure a strict observance, special blackout material had to be affixed to doors and windows. Some women earned a small income by running it up on their Singer sewing machines.

The blackout was intended to make it difficult for enemy aircraft on night raids. My younger brother, Joseph was born shortly before this stage of the war. Whenever an air raid took place, he and I huddled together with Mam in a cupboard beneath the stairs, the close proximity to one another giving a sense of comfort in the face of danger. The cupboard under the stairs would have afforded very little protection in the event of a direct hit, and it was not long before we were issued with a steel table-shelter. The kitchen was not big enough to accommodate it, so it was put in the front room. A tablecloth and a vase of flowers gave it a homely appearance; at night, whenever danger threatened, we got underneath it. Alerted by the fearful wail of the siren, I would be ushered into the front room, or brought from my bed if the hour was late. In the ensuing silence, we listened apprehensively for the ominous drone of approaching aircraft. Faint at first, it gradually grew louder until they seemed to be directly overhead. Then came a series of dull thuds of varying intensity, and intermittent flashes which lit up the night

The author and Joseph.

sky. Trembling, we listened to the German bombs pounding Sunderland eight miles away. Though places nearer home such as Cornwall, the Waterworks, and the port of Seaham, three miles distant, were bombed, Sunderland received greater attention; yet, incredibly, all the shipyards escaped serious damage.

After the last bomb had been heard detonating, there followed another interval of silence, and Mam's voice would be heard, gently reassuring, 'There now, they've gone. It's all over.'

The relief was palpable when, as if in confirmation of Mam's assurances, the self-same siren, no longer a thing of dread but now a welcome sound, signalled the 'All Clear.'

One night, an explosion shook the house. 'That's in Murton,' Mam said fearfully.

Dad disagreed: 'It's miles away.'

Perhaps he was genuinely mistaken, or perhaps it was his way of calming the situation. Princess Street lay diagonally opposite the pit gates, and with about 120 houses was the longest street in Cornwall. The bomb had fallen on the middle of the street, reducing several houses to rubble and killing the occupants.

The neighbourhood positively buzzed one fine, clear morning, as a crowd of about thirty youngsters milled about in the street, talking excitedly.

'Are you comin'?' Ivan Stobie asked me, as I left the house by the back door.

'Where to?'

'Over the line. A German plane has been brought down in a field.'

I didn't hesitate. It was a two-mile trek over the fields to the railway line; it would be worth it just to see the wrecked plane, but I imagined us poring over the wreckage, finding all kinds of fascinating items to be added to our collections, including an abundance of aeroplane glass. In our morbid quest for souvenirs it is doubtful if very many of us spared a thought for the unfortunate pilot and crew.

I didn't bother asking my parents' permission – it was not likely to have been given – so I was one of a boisterous, indisciplined battalion of boys, that set off for the railway line, led by the older ones in the street, such as Ivan and Jimmy Grieveson. After traversing the first field, we came to a leafy beck; by following the beck upstream we eventually arrived at its source in a patch of marshland. From here, we had only to negotiate another field before arriving at the railway embankment. The gradient of this last field was fairly steep, so the embankment atop of it rose up before us like the plateau of a small mountain.

Approaching it breathless, we spied ragged companies of boys coming from other directions from other parts of Murton. The line was already crowded with them; their loud, excitable voices had been clearly audible while we were still some way off. Eagerly, we scrambled up the embankment and pushed our way through the crowd. The landscape beyond the embankment was dominated by Slingley Hill Farm, whose farm buildings sprawled along the summit of the hill. The downed plane, having missed these, lay not fifty yards from where we now stood; the main body was more or less intact, and smaller wreckage was scattered on the lower slope of the hill. Our information had been only partly true: it wasn't a German plane at all, but one of ours. The dead pilot, it was later rumoured, had been thrown clear of the cockpit and, still occupying his seat, was discovered in a nearby hedge. What is certain is that all the crew members lost their lives. The aircraft was an Armstrong Whitworth Whitley AD685, and had been on a solo cross country flight when the tail and part of the wings had become disconnected.

Further progress was impeded by the presence of the police, who were firmly in control. The wrecked plane was tantalizingly close, but the police were not about to allow hordes of children to go foraging among the wreckage. Pleas of 'Aw gawn, let us' and complaints that it was 'not fair' were met with an unsympathetic shake of the head and a firm injunction to 'Go home!' In those far-off days, children respectfully submitted to authority, and two or three policemen were more than enough to hold an army of restless juveniles at bay. After remaining long enough to satisfy our curiosity there was nothing for it but to return home. The scar left on the landscape by the broken aircraft was visible long after the wreckage had been removed.

Murton miners were mostly family men, and when they went out socially more usually it was in the company of their wives. Mam and Dad were keen picturegoers, and since they always took me with them, I grew up with a fervent interest in the pictures myself. At the outbreak of war, the risk posed by air raids decided the government to close the cinemas. The order was soon rescinded when it was judged that the benefits to morale by keeping them open far outweighed any risk.

In the dark days of the war, the pictures provided a welcome doze of escapism. It was probably this need for escapism, and not the lack of any critical or aesthetic sense, that made Abbott and Costello Hollywood's best-loved war-time export, and the one guaranteed to pack the cinema every night they appeared.

Wartime films, of whatever genre, frequently made propaganda statements favourable to the Allies – the Sherlock Holmes mysteries often ended with one. Films about the war itself were, of course, blatantly propagandist, and highly effective. We seethed with fury when sinister-looking Japanese sprang gleefully from ambush to bayonet wholesome young Americans in the back. It was possible to justify the portrayal of the Japanese in this way by claiming that the characterization was consistent with events, and by pointing to the fact that metaphorical back-stabbing was exactly the tactic Japan had deployed against the Americans at Pearl Harbour. Oriental-American actors, Richard Loo and Philip Ahn were called upon throughout the 1940s to reprise their stock role of the urbane Japanese authority figure of fiendish duplicity, who we all loved to hate. As we did the new persona of Chinese actor, Keye Luke, familiar to cinema audiences everywhere as jaunty, wide-eyed number one son of Charlie Chan, now metamorphosed, in accordance with war-time requirements, into a sly, narrow-eyed Japanese thug.

Because the Germans were the original enemy, and possibly because the Luftwaffe's nightly visits brought them closer to home, they rather than the Japanese became the bogeymen of childhood. It was Germans who were waiting at the top of the stairs, or hiding inside the wardrobe in the corner of the bedroom, so you pulled the blankets over your head to shut them out. Their leaders personified evil – Hitler, Goebbels, Goerring, the sound of their names was sufficient to inspire dread.

In 1944, the war was at last going the Allies way. In June, the combined operation for the liberation of Europe began with the Normandy landings. In Burma, the British 14th Army inflicted the first major defeats on the Japanese army at Imphal and Kohima. Returning home from school one lunchtime, I was surprised to see my grandmother. She was wearing her pinny but no coat. She and my mother were crying. Grandma had received a telegram, and had immediately dropped everything and run with it to our house, not even bothering to put on her coat. The brevity of the words no less than the bleak message they contained must have been a leaden weight in the hearts of the two women: 'I regret to inform you that your son, Corporal Joseph Slater is missing in action, presumed dead.' The words would be tragically familiar to thousands of wives, mothers and sisters; only the names differed. There was great loss of life at Imphal and Kohima. The Japanese suffered most, losing over half their forces, but British losses totalled almost 17,000 men. The day Uncle Joe parked his tank in our back street to sit down and eat at our kitchen table was the last we saw of him.

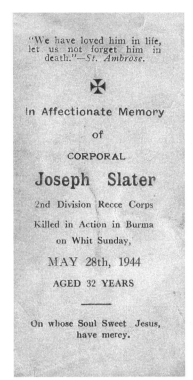

Uncle Joe's memorial card.

My youngest brother, Kevin was born in the last year of the war. After two boys, my mother's dearest wish was to have a girl. Her wish appeared to have been granted when the midwife, concerning whose abstemiousness my mother and grandmother had long had their doubts, announced the birth of a beautiful baby girl. The sound of congratulations had hardly died away before my grandmother peered into the cot and, casting a knowing eye over the infant's nether parts, sniffed disdainfully, 'That baby's a boy.' Mam quickly got over her disappointment, however, and the new arrival was showered with love.

Mam could not bring herself to share in the euphoria that took place at the end of the war, though, like everyone, she was glad that the war was over. The celebrations in Trafalgar Square and elsewhere, seen on the newsreels, only brought tears to her eyes. She had lost her only brother, and my grandparents their only son. It was Vera's loss too, though, thankfully, her husband, Albert, returned safely from overseas. No doubt there were countless others who did not feel in a celebratory mood.

For me, it was an earlier event that provided the most poignantly symbolic ending to the war, though at the time hostilities were still going on. It was a night time, and a curious atmosphere pervaded the house. Everyone seemed elated for some reason; not so much Dad, but my mother and grandmother seemed hardly able to contain themselves.

'Come and see. Hurry, now!' Mam said, indicating that I should go at once to the front door.

'Be quick! Outside!' Grandma registered her impatience when I hesitated.

I hadn't the faintest idea what it was about, but the four of us went out the front door and on to the garden path. There, the adults stood aside and allowed me to walk to the gate alone. The first thing I noticed was how unusually bright it was out; a sky full of stars could not have shed that much light. I paused at the gate and gazed, awestruck, at a row of lighted streetlamps extending the length of the street.

I suppose the end of the blackout was marked in much the same way throughout the country. It is faintly whimsical, in retrospect, to imagine parents everywhere shepherding their children out into the night so they could stand and gawk at the street lighting. The wonder in the eyes of children of the war years at seeing the world at night lit up again, or perhaps at seeing it lit up for the first time, must have been a touching sight; and the eagerness of their parents not less so.

Uncle Joe's grave.

A MIDDLING SCHOLAR

Father Conway – an influential figure and occasional school visitor.

The war was hardly over before there was a General Election. The General Election seemed a fitting postscript to the war: it denoted a return to normality; business as usual, it seemed to say.

Local MP Manny Shinwell.

The first I knew of it was when Arnie Gruthious jumped on me in the school field, grabbing my shirt collar. 'Who do you support, Shinwell or MacMillan?' he growled menacingly.

The names were as familiar to me as those of Nietzsche and Schopenhauer; still, I had a fifty-fifty chance of getting it right. 'Shinwell,' I said, and held my breath. The expected tortures never came. Instead, I was congratulated on the soundness of my politics and set free. The General Election had quickly been perceived as a matter of importance, and a good excuse for the older lads to flex their muscles and teach the younger lads who was boss. All over the playing field, youngsters were being accosted and having the same question put to them that had been put to me. I felt a trifle smug at having guessed right, seeing that others were not so lucky. When next challenged, I confidently proclaimed my support for Mr Shinwell, only to learn, after much agonizing arm-twisting, that Toryism, too, had its supporters in Murton St Joseph's School.

I was by this time a junior in Miss Madigan's class. Miss Madigan was the oldest teacher in the school and a noted disciplinarian. I was now reading and writing fluently, and my numeracy skills had progressed to the level of long division and long multiplication. I held my own in class during the oral part of the lesson, but could not compete with the likes of Paddy Doyle, who was always ready with quick answers and the first to put his hand up. Paddy Doyle was the class extrovert, who had a penchant for routinely interjecting into conversations miscellaneous items of knowledge that he had picked up, and which no one else knew. He was admired for his nerve, and for possessing a flair for occasional outrageous behaviour. In his last year at school, he once appeared wearing a hand-painted tie displaying a nude figure. Of course, he was promptly made to remove the tie, but the incident served its purpose in making Paddy the talk of the school.

Miss Madigan marked all work at her desk, where each pupil in turn stood in nervous expectation while she marked it. A tick with her pen would be made against every sum correctly done. After a brisk series of red ticks had been made down the right hand side of the page, the tension eased and you began to congratulate yourself on getting them all right. When, however, she paused, pen suspended, you held your breath. If a cross was put against a sum, her hand would come up to grab a handful of hair and your head would be pulled down to the level of the exercise book.

'You've put that six in the wrong column, haven't you?'

'Yes, Miss.'

'Yes, Miss, indeed. Because you weren't paying attention when I was at the blackboard, were you?'

'No, Miss – I mean, Yes, Miss.'

'What, then? Downright carelessness, I suppose?'

'Yes, Miss.'

'Do the sum again.'

'Yes, Miss.'

Another device of hers, reserved for the habitually obtuse, was to enunciate arithmetical formulas, punctuating each syllable by the application of her knuckles to the temple. Communicated in this way, when you borrow you must pay back was a reminder more likely to induce amnesia than cure it. This she did, presumably in the belief that when synaptic transmission failed, a forced entry into the brain could thus be effected, and the salient point of the lesson thus assimilated. The futility of the belief was shown by the fact that the same people returned time after time to have their temples knuckled.

St Joseph's being a Catholic school, we were honoured by the sporadic and impromptu appearances of the parish priest, Fr Conway. Father was a local man, born in Hartlepool and educated at Ushaw. Before coming to Murton, he had served in another colliery parish and had been a hospital chaplain. His unexpected entry into the classroom triggered an instant scraping of feet as the class rose as one, loudly intoning a respectful 'Good Morning, Father!' Standing over six feet tall, his Chestertonian bulk clothed in a well-worn clerical suit, Fr Conway easily attracted the eye. Closer inspection revealed greying hair atop heavy, florid features, and a carelessness about cigarette ash decorating his waistcoat.

Father's visits never lasted longer than a few minutes and could be described as being broadly pastoral. A forest of hands would go up in gleeful response to his every question, though his question and answer sessions were diverting rather than educational – 'And what are you studying today, then? The Vikings, eh. And where did the Vikings come from? Russia – is that right, Miss Madigan? But, er, does anyone know what they looked like? Who can tell me that?' And everyone would be shouting 'Father! Father!' at the tops of their voices and straining on tip toe hands held aloft to gain his attention; Miss Madigan would be beaming and the din would be deafening. He once asked the class to guess his weight, and after negating several wild miscalculations, most of them on the short side, presented a two-shilling piece to the girl who came closest.

I served Mass for Fr Conway throughout most of my schooldays. It was at that time obligatory to fast from midnight in order to receive Holy Communion, so when it was my week to serve Mass, I had my breakfast in school before lessons began. After church, I obtained boiling water from the school kitchen to add to the cocoa and sugar in my can, and ate my sandwiches and drank my cocoa at my desk. On rare occasions, the whole school attended Mass and breakfasted in this way, excepting those pupils under the age of seven, who had not yet made their first Holy Communion.

School dinners were introduced when I was in Miss Madigan's class. They were cooked at a central kitchen and delivered to the school kitchen in metal containers. Local women were employed as dinner ladies, and they served the food. In theory, it was a good idea: schoolchildren could have at least one nutritious meal every schoolday at only minimal cost to their parents. The dinner money was collected weekly by the class teacher after registration.

The most favourable comment I can make about school dinners is that they probably were nourishing, if you could force yourself to masticate and swallow without regurgitating copious amounts of mashed potato studded with grey, green, and black lumps, and generous servings of gristle disguised as meat. For years, my only experience of curry was the curried gristle served once a week from the

The author's school report.

school kitchen. It was only when I discovered oriental food much later that I realized that what had passed for curry on the school menu was an even greater travesty than I had originally supposed.

One way you could tell the materially better-off children from the not-so-well-off was in their respective attitudes to school dinners. Some wolfed them down, then sat on the edge of their seats, one foot in the aisle, like sprinters waiting for the starting pistol, before the signal was given for second helpings, when, plate in hand, they would make a bolt for the front. Others, like myself, waited until the serving of dinner was over, then with the same alacrity headed for the swill bucket to surreptitiously scrape their plates clean before the teacher who was supervising could notice.

When it came to the sweet course, however, I was easily pleased, and couldn't get enough of ginger pudding, chocolate pudding, spotted dick, fruit tarts and prunes, and the liberal amounts of custard or white sauce that were ladled over them. Semolina was the one sweet I couldn't stomach, so on semolina day I went home from school half-starved, and compensated at tea-time with more than the usual helping of bread and jam.

School broke up for dinner at mid-day and lessons didn't begin again until 1.30, leaving an hour and a half of free time. Trevor Nares, one of the bigger lads, was friendly with me, and also with the dairyman who delivered milk from the dairy farm. Trevor travelled the milk round with the dairyman and his assistant during the dinner break, and, to my huge delight, gained permission for me to join them. I can recall no greater thrill as a boy. To race out of school and see the little milk cart parked at the school gates waiting for me was heaven. It was a light, two-wheeled cart with a step at the back for boarding and unboarding. What with the four of us and the milk churns there wasn't much room behind the horse. The horse trotted along at an easy gait and, being familiar with the route, needed little prompting. Trevor and I didn't do much, but just rode on the cart. Sometimes the dairyman allowed me take the reins, and to say 'Whoa, there!' when we had to stop at the door of a customer, and 'Giddup!' when we wanted to move on. It was a tremendous thrill to get the horse to obey me in that way. Once, when I was left alone on the cart, something spooked the horse and it took off, leaving the reins trailing on the ground and empty milk churns lying in the road in its wake. Horse and cart, with me desperately hanging on, had gone more than a hundred yards up the street before the dairyman caught us up and managed to calm the horse. I thought it would be the end for me, but the dairyman was a placid sort, quite unable to say a harsh word to anyone. I continued to ride the milk cart until Trevor lost interest or found something else to do with his time; after that, I didn't feel able to continue myself, as I was never on such intimate terms with the dairyman as Trevor had been.

The two play yards at the front of the school were separated by high iron railings. The girls' yard was paved and therefore ideal for the kind of games girls played, such as statues and hitchy dabbers, known in foreign parts as hop scotch, and skipping with one at each end of the rope and the rest taking it in turns to run in. The boys' yard was covered in gravel, and this accounted for the grazed knees and elbows, which were always very much in evidence. We played some rough games in the yard, such as Cockarooso, and Deliver, and a particularly violent version of football.

Football was played on the school field if a real football or casey could be obtained; if not, as was more often the case, and someone had a small ball, a game might be organized in the yard, using the school gates as one goal and forming the other under the window of Big Gal's classroom, using little piles of coke as the goalposts. The pieces of coke came from the mountain of coke which was always lying outside the school boiler-room. This proved to be a particular inconvenience as it hampered the efforts of the left winger on the side kicking up the yard. The iron railings were another hindrance, as people crashed against them while hacking the shins of the person in possession of the ball. Some of the rails were damaged and stuck out dangerously at the bottom.

Once, tired of tripping over and grazing my shins on one particularly vicious rail, I got down on my hands and knees to wrestle furiously with it in an attempt to force it back into line. Alas, I succeeded only in disconnecting a rusting bolt, so that instead of being realigned, the rail now hung loose at an angle. I was studying the bolt, wondering what to do with it, when I became aware of a large shadow darkening my field of vision. Glancing up, my eyes met the stern gaze of Big Gal. She had never before had occasion to even notice me; now I cowered before this towering ogress.

'What's that you are doing?' she demanded.

'Nothing, Miss.'

'Why aren't you playing with the others?'

Before I could reply, her eye caught the rusting bolt which I still held in my hand. 'What's that in your hand?'

'Please Miss, it's a bolt,' I managed to mumble.

She paused before giving me a pitying look. 'Little things amuse little minds,' she said imperiously, and lumbered on her way.

I could have cried with relief. I had been caught out in an act of vandalism by the most feared teacher in the school, and might have expected, if not summary execution, then chastisement of a particularly nasty sort. Instead, I had gotten clean away, having been pronounced an imbecile. What joy! Not wishing to chance my luck further, however, I made sure I kept well out of her way for the next few days.

Perhaps the greatest risk of injury attended the game of Mounty Kitty, which always took place in the playing field against the perimeter fence. Two teams were involved. One team's anchor man stood with his back to the fence, his arms supporting the upper body of the boy in front. This person would bend forward from the waist so that his head fitted snugly into the anchor man's midriff. Each of his team-mates would put his head between and clasp his arms around the thighs of the boy in front. The human chain thus formed had to be vaulted over by members of the other team, their object being to make the line collapse. Those forming the chain had to stand firm until the last jump had been taken and a simple ditty had been recited: 'Mounty Kitty, Mounty Kitty, one, two, three (repeat) one, two, three.' The easiest way to bring about a collapse was first, to aim at the smallest, weediest boy in the line, then to get the maximum height possible in the jump, holding the legs behind the knees on descent so that impact was made with the heaviest part of the body, and, finally, to come down on the weakest spot, that is, where the neck of the weediest boy abutted the buttocks of the boy in front. Every member of the chain had to keep his legs rigidly straight for the duration; once the knees began to buckle, there was no hope of avoiding a collapse. It was a rough game, but schoolboys are a tough breed, and only rarely were injuries incurred.

Due entirely to my mother's diligence, I was almost never late for school. My attendance record was likewise faultless, excepting only when I fell victim to one of those periodic visitations of contagion known as childhood diseases. Less common today, the group included measles, mumps, whooping cough, chicken pox, scarlet fever and yellow jaundice, and chicken pox and scarlet fever were the only two I managed to avoid. Some, like scarlet fever and measles, had once been feared for their plague-like virulence and high mortality rate; but if at one time you would have been quarantined and had your house burnt to the ground, catching them now was all a part of growing up.

Young lads in the 1960s recreate the old game of Mounty Kitty.

It was diphtheria and TB that people commonly feared. Several of Dad's cousins met a premature death, having fallen victim to TB. Small children, particularly, fell prey to diphtheria; the epidemic of the early 1940s claimed the life of the little boy whose back door faced our back door, and that must have made it a worrying time for my parents and the parents of other children living close by.

Minor medical problems meant a visit to the doctor's, accompanied by my mother. Dr McKinnon had his surgery on the Terrace. Beyond the front door, a glass-panelled inner door opened on to a sparsely furnished waiting room. Somehow this was always full, no matter what time you arrived. No appointments were ever made, and there was no receptionist to report to before the doctor dealt with your complaint. You showed up at the surgery on the day your symptoms manifested your lack of health and took your turn in the waiting room, where you found a space on the bench that ran along two abutting walls. When the last person who was in the waiting room when you arrived had been in to see the doctor, you knew it was your turn.

Once I was led into the doctor's presence, my mother would give him an account of what was wrong with me, and then have me confirm that her summation was correct. After a cursory examination, his first question was almost always 'What colour is his water?' This could range from amber to brown with several shades of green in between. Anything approximating brown was bad. When my mother had told him, and he had elicited from me all other relevant information, he would nod sagely, and perhaps suggest a few days off school, to my secret delight. Then from the variously-coloured bottles that filled the shelves from ceiling to floor of his surgery, he would take what he required to make up the medicine appropriate to my condition. Cough mixture, tonic, cures for diarrhoea, loss of appetite, chronic indigestion and a hundred other ailments were to be obtained from the bottles on those shelves. Dr McKinnon never wrote a prescription for me, or for anyone else that I knew of, but whatever medicines my ailments required he dispensed himself.

Childhood diseases entailed perhaps a week in bed followed by a week or two of convalescence. Once the fever stage had passed, I found being laid up in bed pleasurable, in a perverse way, principally as relieving me of the necessity of attending school; but for other reasons too. It was nice to be made a fuss of, to have my meals brought to my room, and be allowed plentiful drinks of lucozade, which was only ever bought when I was sick.

The pleasure derived from not having to go to school was fine for a while; but negative freedom, in the sense of a lack of constraint, and, more importantly, purpose, can be as debilitating as disease itself. The tedium of solitary excursions into the street soon became too much. I missed my schoolfriends, even if I did not miss school. The shrill voices heard coming from the schoolyard every playtime and lunchtime made me conscious of a strange yearning, and I wasn't altogether sorry when the time came to return to school.

CHURCH

A Sunday Evening Procession from St Joseph's Church. The priest is the curate, Fr Richard Cass.

'Pat, are you up yet?' A pause. 'It's five minutes past eight. If you don't get out of bed soon you'll be late for church!' It is Dad shouting up from the bottom of the stairs, in a vexed mood, for it is the second time I have been called.

This scene took place every Sunday morning. Whoever said that religion is a crutch didn't know what he was talking about. If you live your religion, you take up a cross not lean on a crutch. Rising at eight on a Sunday morning and going without breakfast until past ten-thirty, at which time many I knew would be reading the papers in bed with a mid-morning cup of tea, was a modest enough cross to bear, especially when my parents got up earlier and fasted longer; but having had to rise at the same time for school five days a week, it was a cross nevertheless.

The Methodists had a place of worship in Murton from the time the pit was sunk, and at one time it was possible to count three Methodist chapels. Anglicans were at first served by St Andrew's Church in nearby Dalton-le-Dale, before the foundation, in Murton, of the parish church of Holy Trinity. Pentecostalists and Salvationists were also well established among the worshipping community; a circular stone above the brick entrance to the Salvation Army Citadel bears a foundation date of 1900.

Murton Catholics at first walked over the fields to neighbouring Easington to attend religious services. When the school opened in 1899, it served also as a chapel, to which missionary priests came on horseback from Easington to say Mass and to administer the sacraments. A few years later, St Joseph's became a Catholic parish in its own right with its resident parish priest.

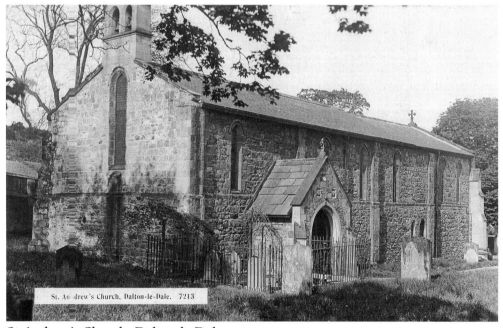

St Andrew's Church, Dalton-le-Dale.

St Joseph's Church, viewed from the graveyard.

The first church was a prefabricated one, which had previously belonged to a parish in Northumberland; it was situated across the road from the school, within its own, quite extensive, grounds. These included a graveyard and a vegetable garden, used by the school. To walk up to it from the main road, you followed a winding path which took you past the parish war memorial, the outstanding feature of which was a life-size crucifix.

The interior of the church was surprisingly spacious, and wonderfully ornate, with its elaborate high altar, stations of the cross, and other statuary, and its abundance of candles, a characteristic feature of Catholic churches. The church was left open during the day for the benefit of worshippers who may have been passing by and wished to call in to offer a prayer, or to spend a few moments in quiet contemplation. At school, we were encouraged to pay regular visits during the lunch break. It was peaceful sitting alone in the quiet of the church when outside the wind was rustling the leaves and causing the boughs to creak, sometimes to be warmed by sunbeams, which came slanting through the stained glass windows to bathe the interior in a myriad mottled colours. Two side aisles flanked the nave of the church. On Sunday, the whole of this section would be filled with schoolchildren; as an expression of solidarity, and also to ensure the maintenance of order, the teachers from the school sat with their respective classes, where they occupied the end seats next to the aisle. Grown-ups filled the pews of the side aisles.

St Joseph's had a good choir, thanks largely to the efforts of Jimmy Rankin, who had taken over as organist and choirmaster on his return from war service, but due also to the quality of some of the choristers. One of the tenors was my uncle, Jimmy Green, who was married to Aunt Jennie, Dad's sister, and who had once performed professionally, or, as Dad put it, had once trod the boards.

It was an habitual practice in Fr Conway's time, and one that his parishioners had come to accept as more or less normal, that Sunday services always began twenty minutes later than the advertised time. Mass-goers living half-a-mile from the church could leave the house at five minutes past nine and, travelling on foot, still arrive in good time for nine o'clock Mass. Unfortunately, the precedent that gave rise to this grotesque logic, once it was established, was nigh impossible to reverse. But such foibles only go to show that priests, like the rest of us, are human; and if anyone gave much thought to the matter, the thought would more likely have been accompanied by a secret chuckle and a wry shake of the head, as much as to say, well, that was Fr Conway for you.

The interior of St Joseph's Church.

The church was always full way beyond its capacity for nine o'clock Mass. Often, Fr Conway would invite the schoolchildren to leave their seats and sit on the altar steps or on the floor at the front, to make room for the adults standing at the back of the church, who had arrived late and were unable to find seats. Whenever this happened, my brother, Joseph and myself had strict instructions from Dad to remain where we were. As he said, we were up early and in good time for church, and he refused to allow us to give up our seats to those 'too lazy to get out of bed on a Sunday.' Consequently, Joseph and I would be the only children left sitting in the middle section of the church, in fearful and, until the rest of the seats had been filled up by the adult late-comers, conspicuous rebellion. Were we to be challenged for our lack of co-operation in the matter, most likely to have been by our class teachers if anyone, then we were both well-drilled in the response we were to make – simply to refer them to Dad, who doubtless would have taken great pleasure in setting them straight on the matter. However, no one ever questioned our behaviour; Dad continued to make his point, or, to be precise, Joseph and I continued to be instrumental in making it for him, and I am fairly sure it did not go unnoticed.

As many could testify, Fr Conway was an extremely witty after-dinner speaker. He was a much less accomplished performer in the pulpit, however, where his delivery suffered from much hesitancy and some amount of throat-clearing. To be fair to him, this was not so much in evidence when he was preaching his homily, as when he was appealing for money. It used often to be remarked, not least by Catholics themselves, that Catholic priests were always asking for money for one cause or another. The foremost cause in our case was that of a new and permanent church, and it was to this end that all Fr Conway's hopes and efforts were directed, and was the reason why, as my mother shrewdly observed, he went about in a suit with frayed cuffs. It was also my mother who, in her succinct way, put her finger precisely on Fr Conway's predicament: 'He can't beg,' she reflected ruefully.

When Mass was over, the congregation poured out into the churchyard from doors at the front and back of the church. Smokers lit up; schoolfriends met up again, and men stood in small groups and discussed the Sunderland game of the day before. At the conclusion of 11 o'clock Mass, many would head for the Big Club, the Demi, or the High House to work up an appetite for dinner. It was usual for members of whichever of the parish groups had priority to assemble in the church hall after the late Mass for their monthly meeting.

To the left of the church as it was approached from the main road, stood the fine, stone presbytery, home of the parish priest. Standing in the shadow of the presbytery was the somewhat dilapidated church hall. High, wide-branched trees, heavy with foliage throughout half the year, screened out much of the daylight, giving the building a forlorn appearance and making it necessary to have the lights on day or night, whenever it was in use.

The interior was roughly pyramidal in shape, high and spacious in the middle, with a pitch to the ceiling at both ends. Everyone on entering had to duck and walk with head and shoulders bowed until the ceiling levelled out so as to accommodate the upright form. It rained in here and there, and could be draughty and cold in winter, despite the presence of an old-fashioned stove; but even in winter, on heady nights, when with shouts and laughter reels and quadrilles were performed in time to music, the little hall generated its own heat. Many a would-be Fred Astaire had taken his first dance steps at a church social held there. It had a good floor for dancing, but being only about sixty feet in length and a few feet across, it was really not adequate for the big occasion. Seating along three walls put a further limitation on space.

The hall was once the lively scene of a boys' club, which met twice-weekly in the evening. There was great enthusiasm for it to begin with; while it functioned it was somewhere for us to go at nights as an alternative to the pictures or the street. Arnie Gruthious had a hand in running it, sometimes assisted by one or two of the older lads, who, like Arnie, had left school and were now working. I contributed my shilling a week, like everyone else, and the first equipment we bought after we had accumulated a large enough sum were several pairs of boxing gloves.

To form the boxing ring, everyone had to join hands and make a circle in the centre of the floor. Unfortunately, every time the circle broke the two contestants ended up brawling in every part of the hall. People wearied of constantly having to pull them apart and restore order to the contest. A modified game of cricket was played, using an upended stool as the wicket, and for a while this proved more popular than the boxing.

Arnie knew a few games of a sadomasochistic type. One, particularly, was memorable for its unrestrained use of a leather belt. Everybody stood in a circle facing inwards and bending forward from the waist, hands held open at the back. Arnie then quietly circled the group several times, before secretly depositing the belt in someone's hand. Whereupon this person, after stealthily withdrawing from the group, proceeded to flog his nearest neighbour round and round the circle of cheering boys. While the game caused huge delight, the red weals across legs and thighs bore graphic testimony of the pain endured by those on the receiving end.

Inevitably, interest in the boxing faded; lacking the necessary skills, and the expert instruction needed to acquire them, people tired of merely trading punches; and the impracticality of playing cricket in such a confined area became evident once the first window had been demolished. After a while, even Arnie's dubious recreations lost their fascination. Boredom set in, attendances dropped, the two nights a week became one night; finally, after being in operation for no more than a few weeks, the club folded.

After many years as an altar boy, the occupation became second nature to me. But there was a time, very early, when disaster attended almost my every effort. At first, I managed quite well, because usually there were two other servers, both older than me, whose greater experience helped me along. Reciting Latin phrases, I discovered, wasn't too difficult when done in conjunction with others. Then, one morning, the other two unexpectedly failed to turn up. By the time Fr Conway had donned his vestments for Mass and was on the point of leaving the vestry for the altar, it dawned on me that I was his sole altar server.

Making the sign of the cross at the foot of the altar steps, Fr Conway intoned the opening words of the Mass: 'Introibo ad altare Dei – I will go up unto the altar of God.' Pausing, he awaited my response. At that moment, I became suddenly, inexplicably, mute. For some reason, the words wouldn't come. Behind me, a congregation waited. Every statue and painted image seemed to hang on my expected utterance.

Fr Conway, looking faintly puzzled, peered down at me from above. 'Ad deum ...' he prompted.

'Ad deum ...' I heard myself repeat the words.

'qui laetificat ...'

'qui laetificat ...'

'juventutem meam ...'

'juventutem meam ...'

And so it continued, until the long liturgy of the beginning of the Mass was completed.

Not long after my bout of liturgical stage fright, I again disgraced myself, and caused widespread alarm among the people in the congregation, when I accidentally set myself on fire.

It was on a Thursday evening, before the commencement of the service of Benediction, when the church was about a quarter full. It was my responsibility to take a taper and light the altar candles. The candelabrum on the side altar was triangular, with candles ascending on two sides to a single, topmost candle. The habitual, and commonsensical, practice was to light the topmost candle first, and then the others in descending order. Unthinkingly, I proceeded to light them from the bottom up. I was straining to reach the last candle, when the quiet of the church was shattered by a sudden explosion of activity. Running in church was never done, not even by small children, as it showed

St Joseph's War Memorial and south end of old church, shortly before they were pulled down to make way for the new church. The little girl is the author's sister, Mary.

a lack of proper reverence; so when I heard the urgent pounding of men's footsteps coming from behind, it was obvious something was amiss.

Mr Kelly reached me first, and immediately began beating me vigorously over the back and shoulder. Instinctively, I shrank away from him. 'Keep still! Don't move!' he urged, as he flapped with his hands against my blazing cotta. Then Mr Wilson arrived from the far side of the church, and he too started laying into me. By the time the flames had been put out, I was feeling rather scared, and not a little foolish. But for the prompt action of the two men I might have been seriously burnt. Just then, the organ started up as Jimmy Rankin tried a few practice chords of *O Salutaris Hostia* – *O Saving Victim*. The service was about to begin. Fr Conway, vested for Benediction, was waiting with the remaining altar boys in the vestry, and, no doubt, wondering as to the cause of the sacrilegious hullabaloo taking place in the church, unaware that a serious conflagration had just been averted.

My mother managed to patch the cotta, which, unfortunately, did not belong to me but to my cousin, Gerard Foley; that involved me in further embarrassment, though Gerard was magnanimous enough not to complain about it.

The church was never more than a third full for Benediction on a Sunday evening, except at certain times in the year when the service included a solemn procession. At such times, people who otherwise never went to Benediction would make the effort to attend, and the church would be full.

A procession is a ceremonial walk which might include the carrying of banners, or, on state occasions, the emblems of state. A religious procession is usually accompanied by the singing of hymns, and is both an act of worship and a public profession of faith. The procession of the Blessed Sacrament was led by the priest, wearing a ceremonial cope and carrying the monstrance containing the consecrated host. Flanked by altar servers carrying candles, and accompanied by the thurifer, he walked beneath an ornate canopy, supported by a pole at each corner borne by members of the congregation. In the Marian month of May, a statue of the Blessed Virgin would be carried in procession, with schoolchildren walking before it strewing rose petals. The church grounds at St Joseph's were traversed by winding paths, bordered by thick bushes and tall trees that met overhead, and thus were eminently suitable for such occasions. After progressing up the aisle of the church, the procession left the church by a side door, then snaked its way around the grounds, re-entering the church by another door. The large numbers of those taking part meant that those at the front of the procession would be re-entering the church as the tail-enders were on the point of leaving it.

Every St Patrick's Day we celebrated our Irishness. For weeks beforehand, the parish school across the road from the church echoed to lusty renditions of *Hail Glorious St Patrick*, and to the more mellifluous cadences of *The Dear Little Shamrock*, as Miss Gibson or

The Miners' Hall (right) – the venue for many celebrations in Murton.

Miss Daly dutifully rehearsed them for the day when they would be sung in church. The St Patrick's Night Dance was by far the outstanding social event of the year. The venue varied: sometimes it was held in the church hall, but this was hardly appropriate considering that many in the parish could be expected to attend, plus a fair number of non-Catholics; so the much more accommodating Miners' Hall or some other suitable venue would usually be booked for the occasion, together with the always reliable Penman family band.

On the morning of March 17th, we would be marched over from school, each class escorted by the class teacher, and, with the adults, would fill the church for Mass and the distribution of shamrock. No one, adult or child, was left without a soggy bunch of shamrock. Trays heaped with the stuff, newly arrived from Ireland, awaited us at the front of the church. Then, with the lush weed and symbol of the triune God sprouting profusely from our coat lapels, we would go forth, a little awed, proud maybe, and, in my case, sometimes sheepishly apologetic on being greeted by a bemused non-Catholic friend with the words, 'Hey, Pat, why are you wearin' that chickenweed in your buttonhole?'

The most solemn and, at the same time, joyous occasion in the year, that requiring the greatest degree of preparation, occurred early in the summer, when the children made their first Holy Communion. Catholic schoolchildren were left in no doubt that this was the most important day in their lives. For several weeks prior to the event, the First Communion class of seven-year-olds would be at the centre of school and parish life. Under the guidance of their class teacher, they would learn how to adopt the appropriate reverential attitude as they approached the altar, and how to compose their thoughts and prayers before and after receiving Communion. As the day drew near, rehearsals would take place, with wafers representing the consecrated host being placed upon the tongue of every child.

On Sunday, long before the start of Mass, every seat in the church would be taken, and the atmosphere charged with an almost tangible expectancy. The school would be opened for the day, where the girls could change out of their everyday clothes and into their First Communion dresses. It was a big day for the teachers in charge, and Miss Daly and Little Gal would be kept busy adjusting veils and ensuring that coronets were on straight, and giving last minute instructions that in all probability had been given a dozen times before.

At the appropriate moment, the first communicants would cross the road from school and enter the packed church in procession, two by two, their voices sweetly singing their own special hymn, *On My First Communion Day*. All eyes would be turned upon them as they proceeded to the seats reserved for them at the front of the church, girls in veils and white dresses, boys in white shirts and red ties, with hair neatly combed. When it came time for Communion, they would progress in orderly file to the altar rail, hands reverently joined, finger to finger, and under the rapt gaze of parents and family, would receive Christ for the first time, really present in the sacrament under the appearance of bread.

At the conclusion of Mass, exuberant parents and well-wishers would collect in the churchyard to offer their congratulations. Photographs would be taken, and First Communion gifts given out, traditionally rosary beads and Mass books. Commemorative certificates would be issued bearing the communicant's name, the date, and the signature of the parish priest; in many cases, these would be framed and hung on the bedroom wall at home. After the close of the celebrations, the girls would change back into their everyday clothes; the First Communion dress would then be taken home and carefully put away in a drawer, perhaps later to be worn by a younger sister, more likely never to be worn again.

A First Communion class from St Joseph's Church.

SECTION SEVEN

YOUNG TEARAWAYS

My boyhood hero – Jimmy Cagney – and the Dead End Kids.

When I was aged about nine, it was decided that I should be given the benefit of piano lessons. In those days, people made their own music, and the piano was a familiar item of furniture in many homes. Mam and Dad always wanted the best for their children, and I think they had visions of me as a distinguished concert pianist who might one day give a recital on the Third Programme or on stage at the Sunderland Empire.

Once this unilateral decision had been taken, a good, second hand piano was acquired for £80, a princely sum then, and Dad arranged for a workmate, Mr Coates, to give me lessons at a shilling a week. By day, Mr Coates was a horsekeeper at the pit; in the evening, he taught piano to aspiring young musicians.

Mr Coates lived in a council house a short walk from where we lived. He was a thick-set man, with a pale complexion and thinning hair, and was a few years older than Dad, which probably made him about fifty.

His music room was always full when I arrived. His pupils sat quietly awaiting their turn, wearing serious expressions, and nursing briefcases or clutching sheaves of sheet music, while Mr Coates devoted his attention to whoever was at the piano. With one exception, all Mr Coates' pupils were girls: I was the exception. With the hopelessness of one who knows his fate is totally beyond his control, I took my place with the rest, and prayed that a power failure might occur, or that Murton might be hit by a comet, before it was my turn at the piano.

For it soon became apparent, to me, and, presumably, especially to Mr Coates, that in terms of musical ability I was a numbskull of the first rank, and that this grand ambition of my parents was a depressing waste of time and money. Entering Mr Coates' house at six on a Tuesday evening was the most miserable moment of my week, leaving it at seven the most ecstatic. Having mastered a few elementary exercises, I seemed utterly incapable of further progress. 'Every Good Boy Deserves Favour,' Mr Coates would intone over my shoulder, thumping the keys for emphasis, and I would nod dully while staring blankly at the keyboard in front of me, fervently wishing I were somewhere else.

For several weeks, I was to put Mr Coates' humour sorely to the test. There were tense moments when I arrived at the usual impasse, my fingers idly poised over the keys, and I thought he must be on the point of exploding. But if he felt his temper rising, he somehow managed to keep it in check. He must have dreaded those Tuesday night sessions almost as much as I did. I marvel that he put up with me for so long. He probably felt obligated to my father. The loss of his shilling a week, I am sure, he would have considered the smallest of worthwhile sacrifices just to be rid of me. When Mr Coates had had enough of my pitiful efforts, I would be dismissed; he would then crook his finger and, to compound my misery, some pig-tailed child prodigy would haul herself up on to the piano stool before executing a number fit to carry off the Tchaikovsky prize.

Mr Coates was no mean pianist himself, and if I proved to be unteachable, at least I was no philistine. I thrilled to hear him perform, as occasionally he did when he was showing his more advanced pupils how a particular piece should be played. He had short, thick fingers, which I thought not very elegant for a pianist.

I saw a lot of Trevor Nares at this time, who, though two years my senior, for some reason attached himself to me. Trevor was a street tough who other street toughs tended to stay clear of. A loyal friend, he would unhesitatingly take on the role of my protector if I was picked on by older boys who I couldn't handle myself. Trevor wasn't Murton-born, but originated from somewhere in Northumberland. Trevor always went 'doon the Terrace' or 'alang the rurrd,' and he referred to his sister, Edith as 'wor Edith,' all of which I found amusing at first, until I got used to his peculiarities of speech. Trevor's father had been crushed by a fall of stone in a Northumberland pit. When they had scraped what was left of him off the ground, the remains were put in a coffin and the lid was screwed down, so Trevor's mother never saw him. She then brought the family to Murton, her place of birth, so she could be near her mother and sister.

Trevor and I ranged far from home, to the woods beyond the Colliery Welfare Park, or to the Store field on the edge of Murton, to wade in the pond and catch sticklebacks in jam jars. The Store field was where the Store horses grazed and roamed free; gallawas, we called them. Big Gal said they got that name because the pit ponies originally came from Galway in the west of Ireland, though others have claimed that they were brought over from Galloway in Scotland.

Behind the Big Club, was a walled-in grassed area known as the ball alley. It had once been used for games of handball, but was now a play

Murton Athletic Youth Club on the Welfare Park.

area for children. In one corner, a number of trees spread their sturdy branches, inviting the attention of tree-climbers, and there wasn't one I hadn't climbed a hundred times, though no matter how high I climbed, Doris Hardy always managed to climb one branch higher. Trevor would swing recklessly from one branch to another, and even jump from one tree to the next like a chimpanzee. Occasionally, he would get a tear in his shirt or in his trousers, his trousers being, as a general rule, already well patched; and more than once he had the wind knocked out of him falling out of a tree, though he would never admit to having hurt himself. Trevor was more dare-devil than anyone I knew, and could do most things better than anyone else, though I bettered him by learning to hang upside down by my legs from the lower branches of trees, which he could never do.

When the nights grew dark, Trevor and I got our thrills annoying people by knocking on their doors and running away. It was a time-honoured pastime of which there were modified forms. By attaching string to the door knockers, it was possible to knock on two or more doors at the same time. Another refinement was to tilt the water barrel against the door, so when the door was opened, the water barrel fell inside and flooded the inside of the house. Only the most unscrupulous resorted to this stratagem.

The two of us took particular pleasure in tormenting Mr Wilkerson, who had a house in the next street to ours. Wilkie was a big, ungainly man of surly disposition, whose loping gait was imitated by youngsters behind his back. He spent his nights at home, after returning from his allotment, where he occupied his spare time tending the show leeks in his leek trench, and feeding them the mixture made according to his secret leek-growing formula. You usually heard Wilkie before you saw him, for he was very loud. Being hot tempered and decidedly not child friendly made him the perfect target for night-time mischief.

First me, then, after a safe interval, Trevor, ventured down Wilkie's garden path to rattle his door knocker before fleeing the scene. Safely hidden behind a privet hedge, we watched with barely suppressed glee as a crimson-faced Wilkie came to the door and, heedless of his neighbours sensibilities, vented his frustration in such an outpouring of invective as to make the devil himself blush. Wondrously eloquent in his rage, Wilkie would favour us with a few blood-curdling options concerning the fate awaiting any delinquent door-knockers unfortunate enough to fall into his hands, of which strangulation was the most humane.

The house two doors below us was occupied by Mr and Mrs Walker, an elderly couple who lived quietly together, keeping very much to themselves. Mrs Walker was plump and homely-looking, and her husband small and spry. Alas, one night, with despicable disregard for their years, I decided it would be a good idea to knock on their door.

Mr Walker must have seen me coming for he was out the door almost before I had let go of the door-knocker. Allowing for his age, Mr Walker was the fastest human I ever encountered. Not that I saw much of him in flight; but I felt him breathing down my neck as I sprinted at the top of my ability just to keep one step ahead of him. He gave me the fright of my young life as he chased me up the front of the street and down the back, and then up and down three or four other streets before finally giving up on me. Then, with head pounding and chest raw and hurting like the devil, I endeavoured to regain my breath.

I was afraid to go home, feeling sure that Mr Walker would have called at our house and informed on me to Dad. What I dreaded most was the shame Dad would make me feel for pestering the old couple. Staying out as late as I dared, I sneaked in the back door, fully expecting Dad to be waiting to deal with me, but nothing was said and everything at home seemed normal. I couldn't understand it, for I felt sure Mr Walker would have recognized me. In future, I was more wary about whose door I knocked on, and I quickened my step and averted my eyes whenever I had to pass Mr Walker's house. 'Never bother anybody in your own neighbourhood,' James Cagney told the Dead End Kids, to which I might add, especially not super fit geriatrics with a lightening turn of speed.

On the way to the woods or the Store field, you had to pass the Colliery Welfare playing fields. Opposite the entrance to the cricket ground, was the blacksmith's shop, where Trevor and I stopped off on many a Saturday morning to watch the blacksmith at work. Mr Sparrow was a second generation blacksmith, having learnt the trade from his father. He was a mild-mannered man of average build, not at all like the popular conception of the burly village blacksmith. He was used to working before an audience, for children were always hanging about the place. The blacksmith's shop was an old brick building with a corrugated roof, dingy and soot-encrusted within, as you might

Horse-drawn carts in Murton Street – a time when a blacksmith was common in every village.

73

expect of a busy forge. An array of formidable-looking implements hung from the walls, and with the furnace lighting the back wall up to the rafters, the scene might easily have conveyed the impression of it being some shadowy and sinister torture chamber. But the friendliness of Mr Sparrow as he went about his work dispelled such notions. As long as they kept their distance, children were tolerated here, and their interest appreciated. Sometimes, if a horse was being shod, a small row of boys would be standing by the door, looking on in respectful silence, and the air would be filled with the pungent smell of burnt hoof. Mr Sparrow would pump the bellows until the furnace glowed bright red and you could smell the heat. When the horseshoe was malleable, it would be retrieved from the furnace with a pair of outsize pincers and further beaten into shape on the anvil, the hammer strikes dully ringing out over the village like some cracked and discordant church bell. It was the kind of defining sound one heard almost every day, like the rumble of coal wagons on the move, familiar, and, in some strange sense, reassuring. With a sudden hissing noise, the shoe would be doused in a bucket of water, before being carefully matched to the horse's hoof. Mr Sparrow would then take a knife to pare the hoof, clasping it tightly against his leather apron and between his legs. Some rough edges would be taken off with the file, and a final fitting of the shoe would be made before the nails were hammered in. Throughout the whole procedure, the horse stood stolidly unconcerned.

Scarcely a hundred yards from the blacksmith's shop was an area of four or five acres of open grassland known as the Demi Field. The Demi club backed on to it, and a row of poplars screened it from St Joseph's churchyard. St Joseph's pupils commonly used the field as a short-cut to school. A wall surmounted by iron railings had to be climbed at the far corner before crossing the road to the school gates. This was made easier after workmen had cut and removed the railings for the war effort. Shortly after the war, prefabs were built on the Demi Field, and we had to get used to seeing paved streets and lamp posts where once grass had grown and young tearaways had played at Cowboys and Indians.

Before the prefabs appeared, there were about two occasions every year when the Demi Field became a show field. It was always a big occasion, when every night for two, or possible three, weeks the field was transformed into a magical world of steam organ music and brightly-lit side shows, of whirling rides and shrieking girls, and throngs of people promenading on grass criss-crossed by electric cables. My favourite rides were the Flying Chairs and the Shuggy Boats, however, there was a limit to how far my pocket money could be spread between two people, for Trevor never had any money himself.

The two of us found alternative amusement in the dark shadows behind the trailers, where the fairground music was partly muted by the incessant hum of outsize generators. Here we wrestled and tumbled on the grass, and crawled about out of sight beneath the trailers. In this dark hinterland behind the show field courting couples kept assignations, laughing and embracing, and seeming oddly indifferent to the curious stares cast at them by a couple of small boys. For a while after the shows had departed, the Demi Field remained a rather desolate place, with only the lingering smell of oil and the odd patch of black grass reminders that they had ever been.

Trevor was great fun to be with, and he and I were best friends for maybe eighteen months before Trevor's mother remarried and moved to the Nack. After that, I hardly ever saw him again.

Late one congenial Friday evening, I became the recipient of a piece of joyous news, and the beneficiary of an unexpected gift. Vera and Albert were visiting, Albert having recently been discharged from the RAF, and they sat chatting with Mam and Dad in the kitchen. It was one of those warm, intimate occasions, when Joseph and I would sit contentedly at the grown-ups' feet, listening to adult talk, and I found myself wishing it could go on for ever.

During a pause in the conversation, Dad casually let slip the news that I would no longer be required to attend Mr Coates' house for piano lessons. I had never made the least effort to disguise my misery, were that possible, when Tuesday evening came around and time for the hated piano lesson; and Mam and Dad knew by now that there was not the remotest chance that their eldest son would ever perform in the concert halls of Europe, or even, for that matter, in the concert room of the Traveller's Rest. It was with an expression of pained resignation, then, that Dad revealed that he had spoken to Mr Coates that very day and had brought my undistinguished career as a musician to a merciful conclusion. The relief with which I received the news can hardly be imagined.

Welcome as this news was, it was promptly relegated to the category of pleasures to be savoured later, after Albert produced the present he had brought me from the Far East – a football. Nobody in the neighbourhood owned a football. It had oriental letters printed across it and, most unusually, was a size seven. Five was the regular size, though in schools football it was usual for a size four ball to be used. That size seven football became something of a local curiosity, and provided hours of pleasure for many in the street for years to come, though the bladder had to be patched a couple of times and the leather casing stitched at least once.

To complete a memorable evening, Vera gave me two chiclets of Beech Nut. After being thoroughly chewed, the gum was put in an egg-cup of water before I went to bed so that it would still be fresh next day. The next day was Saturday. There was the afternoon matinee in the Rex to look forward to; and after that, a game of football in the street or ball alley with my friends, played, not with a spongy or a tennis ball, but with a casey. And I had chewing gum to last me all day long. They were unsophisticated pleasures that cost next to nothing; but no one in Murton went to bed that night in a more rapturous mood, with a heart so brimming over with joy. Unless it was Mr Coates.

Two of Murton's three cinemas, the Rex and the Olympia, put on Saturday matinee film shows for children. I rarely went to the Olympia matinee, which was held in the morning, but I never missed the afternoon show at the Rex. Opened in 1939, the year the war commenced, the Rex was the largest building in Murton. On a Saturday afternoon, every one of its nine hundred seats would be filled for the children's matinee. The price of admission was threepence, and there was invariably a long queue of impatient, raucous youngsters of both sexes waiting to get in.

Staff of the Empire Cinema in 1949. Sydney Richardson is on the left.

The programme began with a two-reel comedy short, typically featuring the accident-prone Andy Clyde, whose life was an unending battle with everyday objects such as kitchen shelves and revolving doors; or henpecked Leon Errol, trying vainly to cope with an improbable series of ambiguous situations which repeatedly landed him in marital hot water. The most unpretentious plots involved a comedy act known as the Three Stooges. They were guaranteed to lift the roof of the house the instant their images were flashed on to the screen. This demented trio of misfits made brutality almost an art form, and for a long time their films were deemed too violent to be shown on television. Fastening bolt croppers to ears and tearing hair out by the roots in handfuls was extreme behaviour, which could appeal only to a perverse and puerile sense of humour. Needless to say, nine hundred pre-pubescent matinee-goers found it uproariously funny.

Next on the bill was the serial. Like all serials, every episode ended on a cliff-hanger that saw the hero facing certain death. This was intended to get us to go back the next week to see how he managed to escape. One of the first serials I recall seeing, was *The Three Musketeers*; not the Dumas story, but a tale of the Foreign Legion, starring a young and relatively unknown John Wayne. Another, *The*

New Adventures of Tarzan, featured tall, soft spoken Herman Brix as Tarzan (Bruce Bennett, as he later became). The serial was made in Guatemala, and had Tarzan battling hundreds of native extras, who all appeared to be about four feet tall.

The matinee concluded with the big picture, a western starring either Wild Bill Elliott or Johnny Mack Brown. It lasted about an hour, and clearly was not made on a budget that went through the roof or with a shooting schedule that ran into months or even weeks. Half a day would be my guess. The location sequences didn't exactly overawe; but if the majority of us were able to work out that the hero was endlessly chased past the same rock formation or the same clump of cacti, nobody seemed to mind.

Before the big picture was shown, Mr Patten, the cinema manager, would ascend the steps at the side of the stage and hold his hands up to obtain order. In appearance, Mr Patten was hard to miss, especially in a pit village like Murton. He was a big man, with silver hair and a ruddy complexion, who habitually wore tweeds and plus fours, and whose sartorial elegance sometimes extended to the wearing of a monocle. Had he been an actor, he would have been perfect for the part of the cantankerous old colonel whose beautiful, self-willed daughter is bent on marrying the penniless slum doctor, instead of wealthy Nob Hill stuffed shirt, Chester Pendlebury III.

To match his silver hair, Mr Patten was blessed with a silver tongue. As we hung open-mouthed on his every word, his voice boomed out over the auditorium a reminder of his solicitousness: 'I went to great lengths and considerable expense to obtain this film, but I finally managed to get it for you.' Pausing only to gauge the extent of our gratitude, he went on to describe the stupendous cinematic classic we were about to see. Every Saturday, Mr Patten promised to have something different for us the following week, a main feature that would eclipse anything we had previously seen and set us talking about it for weeks on end. Waving a forefinger like a baton, and emphasizing every syllable, he would pronounce the solemn warning, 'Believe me, you will not want to miss this film.' His assured manner and authoritative tone of voice won us over, and we would quake at the thought that we might become gravely ill, or die, or that the Rex might burn to the ground before we had a chance to see the film in question. The next week came round and the main feature would be a western starring either Wild Bill Elliott or Johnny Mack Brown.

The problem with the children's Saturday matinee, and, I imagine, children's matinees all over, was that although many were content to sit quietly and be entertained, there were always those whom no romance could captivate for more than a few moments. So you got used to following the soundtrack of the picture against a buzz of conversation of a level that was just tolerable. At times, fights broke out and were stilled by shouts of 'Sit down!' from those in adjacent seats. Alas, there was nothing one could do to guard against the orange peel, apple gowks and half-eaten toffees that intermittently pelted the back of head and neck from behind. Wads of paper, chewed and wet, became ammunition for makeshift catapults. The catapult was simply a length of elastic wound around the middle and index fingers of one hand, or else stretched end to end with the paper wad held between the teeth until released. The distance that could be obtained meant that ordinarily anonymity was assured. But accuracy could not always be guaranteed, and a wad might easily go astray to find an unintended mark, often falling short to connect with someone nearer home. The victim would then clap a hand to the back of his neck before turning to confront the culprit, when an angry exchange would take place.

'Did you fire that?'

'What if Aa did? Want to make something of it?'

'Aa might.'

'Gan on, then.'

'Aa'll get you outside later.'

'Yeah. You and whose army?'

The acrimony reached a stage when the belligerents would be on their feet, fists clenched, and glowering fiercely at one another, each waiting for the other to throw the first punch, before a loud chorus of 'Sit down!' coming from behind forced a cessation, or possibly, postponement, of hostilities.

The balcony extended over roughly a third of the area of the stalls. Anyone occupying a seat beneath the overhanging part could expect to be the victim of no more than the occasional misdirected projectile. Those seated nearer the screen, however, were not only in the line of fire from the rear stalls, but were also the random targets of missiles raining down from the balcony, whose trajectories could be glimpsed in the glare cast by the film projector. When the mayhem got too bad, the house lights would be switched on, so that the on-screen action, for those still intent on following it, was barely discernible. This precipitated howls of protest and a gradual stamping of feet rising to a crescendo, until, for the sake of quiet, the management was forced to extinguish the lights. Sometimes, Mr Patten would come on to the stage to appeal for calm, and would threaten to cancel the special, blockbusting extravaganza that he had arranged to be shown the following Saturday. Usually, we fell for that, and order would be restored.

Immediately the show ended and the lights came on, a series of loud crashes would be heard as the tip up seats were flung back; the double doors of the four exits would then be thrown open, and within minutes the cinema would be emptied and strangely silent. Girls left, either sedately or else in high-spirited mood, some, made the object of playful teasing, offering shrill rejoinders before heading home. Boys galloped off into the sunset astride make-believe horses, firing make-believe six-shooters at one another, that, like the kind used by Wild Bill Elliott and Johnny Mack Brown, never needed reloading.

SECTION EIGHT

SUMMER

*Murton men having a plodge at
Blackpool in 1949 – Joe Leddy, Billy
Purvis and Tommy Greenfield.*

Three years after the war ended, we moved out of our rented accommodation in Coronation Street West and into a new council house in Toft Crescent, on the north side of Murton, overlooking the fields. These were the same fields where, a few years earlier, most of Murton's youth had blazed a trail to see the crashed Armstrong-Whitworth Whitley, and the railway embankment upon which we had stood and gazed at its broken remains was now to become a familiar, everyday sight.

To the rear of Toft Crescent, several acres of open land, with a football pitch where it rose to a summit, could be glimpsed from the back bedroom window; an area that was commonly known as the Cornfield. From my bedroom window at the front of the house, I could make out the buildings belonging to five farms, and over to the north east a stretch of blue sea was clearly visible. It was a landscape endlessly fascinating, and inviting. Within seconds of leaving the house, I could be standing in open country with the sun at my back and, above, a chorus of larks endlessly singing their monotonous sweet refrain. The song, *Oh What A Beautiful Morning* from the new musical, *Oklahoma*, was constantly being aired on the wireless, and fitted my mood perfectly. That summer, there was always a bright golden haze on the meadow, and the sounds of the earth were like music.

Less than a mile from home, was an area of rough grassland, where whinny bushes grew in thick clumps, and cows commonly grazed on its lower slope. A cart track wandered over it down into a valley, where it crossed a stream by an old bridge with wooden handrails. The place was known as Willey's fields and was popular with picnickers. If you followed the course of the stream from the bridge, it soon brought you to a dene thick with hazel and wild garlic, and, half a mile beyond that, to the village of Dalton-le-Dale. At the end of the Ice Age, with the melting of the ice, huge torrents of water had rushed seawards gouging deep furrows in the land, eventually resulting in a coastal region marked by densely wooded ravines of hazel, hawthorn and yew. These lush denes provided pleasant walks for generations of Murtonians, and play areas for youngsters like myself. Throughout the summer months, Mosey Littlejohn from the street, and myself, followed winding trails and indulged in daredevil escapades, crashing headlong past saplings and through bushes while racing down the steep sides of the dene, and swinging fearlessly from the branches of the bigger trees. Sometimes, for a dare, we would leap the beck at its wider points, not always successfully, so that we got used to tramping the dene in squelching wet boots.

Before disappearing into the dene, there was one place where the stream bed widened, and instead of rising vertically, the bank sloped gently upwards on both sides. It was an ideal spot for a bathing hole. There were any number of rocks lying around with which to dam the stream, so in no time at all it was possible to create an expanse of water some twenty yards long by ten across, with a depth at the centre of perhaps four feet.

The Glebe – the countryside was never far away from our pit village.

On a warm day, youngsters in bathing costumes, real ones or makeshift, splashed about or attempted to swim in an increasingly overcrowded pool, as the grown ups relaxed on the flattened grass of the bank top and surveyed with a casual eye the activity taking place in the water. From time to time, children would dash from the water's edge to slake their thirst from pop bottles which had been brought from home, and which, more usually, contained water rather than pop. Most of the bathers were content to plodge; those who attempted to swim would retreat to the less congested part of the pool, at a point where the stream that fed the bathing hole entered it. Here, the reeds grew in sparse clumps and the water was cooler. The sides of the bank for the first few feet consisted of solid clay of a bright yellow colour. As the day wore on, and the number of bathers increased, a distinct discolouration of the water of the bathing hole was noticeable, so that by the end of the day the bathers all appeared to be plodging in custard.

Older boys periodically dammed the stream further into the dene to make a smaller, but much deeper, bathing hole. One day, larking about in foolhardy fashion, I fell in fully clothed. It was before I had learnt to swim, so for a few despairing moments I flailed around in a panic, before somehow managing to reach the opposite bank and haul myself out of the water.

It was a long walk home, which I undertook in an acute state of self-consciousness, as my bedraggled condition drew curious stares from everyone I met on the way. People came to their back gates to peer at me as I passed by in squelching boots and with water dripping off me.

Luckily, the road took me past Tommy Gilroy's house. Tommy must have been alerted by one of his children; he came out into the street, took one look at me and immediately brought me into his home, where, in front of the fire, I had my sodden clothes removed, before being briskly rubbed down with a bath towel. Meanwhile, Mrs Gilroy kept the children out of sight, sparing my blushes. The family was known to me: Tommy and his wife were regular church-goers at St Joseph's, and one of their children, Andrew, was a classmate of mine. It was entirely typical of the couple that they should have responded to my plight in the way that they did.

Tommy was a small, chirpy character, whose preferred headwear, in the days when trilbies were commonly worn for best, was a bowler hat. He was well-known in Murton for two other things particularly: he had a large, adoring family, and always a fund of jokes, which were mostly told against himself. Every time you met Tommy he had a joke to tell. He would apprehend you by grabbing your arm and then make you listen while he told it. Tommy concluded every joke with a prolonged bout of rattling laughter, and his humour was so infectious that regardless of how good the joke was, it was virtually impossible not to join your laughter to his.

Tommy's distinctive comic trait was his poverty. Raising a large brood of children in wartime could not have been easy; Tommy, though, exaggerated his situation for comic effect. Reputedly, he was once seen pushing a hand cart containing odds and ends, and someone enquired if he was collecting firewood. 'No,' said Tommy, 'moving house.' Whether true or not, the story was typical of him. Tommy was for many years the gravedigger at St Joseph's, where his experiences provided the inspiration for much of his humour.

After being thoroughly dried, I was dressed in warm clothes belonging to one of the elder boys, and given a cup of tea before being escorted home by Tommy's eldest son, Jim. Mam was none too pleased when she learned of the incident, and I received a good telling off for falling into the bathing hole and putting Mr and Mrs Gilroy to so much trouble.

On the edge of the Welfare grounds on the other side of Murton, was a small wood of mostly willow and birch called the First Wood. This gradually thinned out into an expansive area, criss-crossed by rough paths and dotted with whinny bushes; we knew it as the Second Wood, though, strictly speaking, it wasn't a wood at all. A more or less direct route between the whinny bushes eventually brought you to the dark and forbidding plantation known as the Third Wood. These woods provided an ideal location for swashbuckling adventures. Here, we fought marauding Indians, shot arrows at the Sheriff of Nottingham's men, and engaged villainous Spaniards and Frenchmen in epic sword fights.

On the far side of the woods, an expanse of fields bordered the neighbouring pit village of South Hetton. It was perhaps indicative of a certain insularity that an adolescent rivalry should have grown up between the South Hetton lads and us, and tall tales were told of battles fought against them and victories won. I was one of about twenty pupils idling on the edge of the First Wood one lunch time when we were joined by a much larger company from the Council School. Soon a crowd of South Hetton lads about half our number emerged unexpectedly from among the trees not a hundred yards from where we stood. Seeing us, they stopped, and, for a moment, each group eyed the other suspiciously. Soon, we were exchanging mild insults. Filled with the courage borne of the knowledge that you outnumber the enemy, we dared them to 'come over here', and they responded with a loud chorus of jeers. But with time running out, they soon retreated into the wood, and we returned to our respective schools. There, for the benefit of those who had not been present, the folklore was augmented with one more colourfully embellished tale of how the South Hetton lads had been vanquished by the Murton lads. Doubtless, the same story was put about in South Hetton with the reverse result.

One Saturday, I roamed further than I had ever gone before, into the Third Wood and beyond, until the trees thinned out and I was standing in a fallow field with the woods behind me. The field shortly disappeared into a wooded hollow which had a beck running through it narrow enough to jump. Spread out before me on the other side, a sea of wheat extended up the crest of a hill, where, I surmised, I would be in view of South Hetton, half a mile away at most. There I intended turning back.

As I reached the top, I came abruptly upon two boys of about my own age. The three of us came to a stop about five feet apart and stared unblinkingly at one another. They had the advantage, territorially and numerically, so I was somewhat apprehensive. The taller of the two frowned as he eyed me up and down. He might have been a little older than me, and was rather bigger, with crude features and bright ginger hair. His associate was a pale, weedy youth, clothed in a thin shirt and ragged trousers, who looked like the most undernourished member of the Dead End Kids. Ginger took his time, curiosity getting the better of animosity, or whatever emotion he was harbouring, though I didn't think it was fear.

'What are you doin' 'ere?' he said roughly, and leaving me in no doubt that I was trespassing on his patch.

'Nothin'. Just walkin.'

There was a pause. 'You from Murton?'

I hesitated, before confessing that I was indeed a Murtonian.

Ginger ran his eye over me again. If I had said I was a Martian, it could hardly have made a greater impression. 'What's your name, then?' he said, his voice mellowing a little. I told him. 'Mine's Johnson,' he said, puffing himself up. 'And 'is name's Crosby – but Aa'm the boss.'

'Let's go home,' Crosby whined, and was rudely told to shut up. His face wore a dull expression, his eyes lacking sparkle. I thought he might be slow in the head.

'Have you heard of Bing Crosby?' said Ginger.

I nodded.

'Well –' he pointed to the other, 'Ee's Bing Crosby's brother.'

If he glimpsed the flicker of doubt which may have crossed my face, he didn't remark on it.

'We were goin' to the woods to play Tarzan,' Ginger explained, dropping a hand to the sheath knife in his belt. 'Can you do Tarzan's call? aa can – listen.'

Whereupon, he threw back his head and, cupping both hands to his mouth, gave vent to an ear-piercing yodel. Two birds flew out of a nearby tree.

'Let's get some spears,' Ginger said, suddenly becoming quite animated. 'Aa knar, let's play sword fightin'.' He danced around, parrying imaginary sword thrusts. 'Have you seen *The Mark of Zorro*? It's the best picture ever. Aa'll be Tyrone Power.'

He unsheathed his knife and we cut ourselves a sword each from a wild rose bush which had sprouted in the hedge between two hawthorns, quickly shaving off the thorns, while Ginger's dull-eyed companion sat in the hedge and drew his knees up to support his chin.

'Ee cannot fence,' Ginger said scornfully.

I tried my sword out, ostentatiously lashing the air with it. There was a slight delay to the proceedings due to the fact that we both wanted to be Tyrone Power, but eventually I gave in and agreed to be Basil Rathbone. 'On guard!' Ginger suddenly exclaimed, as he adopted a pose, bending his knees and extending his sword arm menacingly. The next moment we were duelling furiously back and forth, trampling the wheat underfoot. I put up a good show before allowing Ginger to run me through, when I crumpled up with an agonized sigh and fell to the ground in melodramatic fashion. Ginger was so impressed with my acting, he demanded a reversal of roles. So then I became Zorro, and obliged him in his desire to die, which eventually he did do after a much prolonged bout of histrionics. Following which, he got up and we started all over again.

Now no one, not even the school board man, inspired as much dread as an angry farmer with trespassers in his sights, especially trespassers who were damaging his crops. We had been at it for quite some time, and had made rather a mess of the wheat. I don't recall which of the two raised the alarm, but suddenly the cry went up – 'The farmer!' In one quick glance, we took in this gentleman rapidly descending upon us with raised fists, and, in another, the wooded hollow with the beck running through it, beyond which lay safety. The next instant the three of us were a tangle of limbs as each sought to get a start on the other two. Sheer terror propelled our legs, as the thud of the farmer's boots could be heard coming closer. Every second, I expected to feel his breath on the back of my neck, his steely hand clamp on to my shoulder. Wild-eyed, arms working like pistons, I strove for the hollow, neck and neck with Ginger. Bing Crosby's brother was across the beck and up the other side before either Ginger or myself had gained the edge of the field. Whether or not he was slow in the head, he was certainly fleet of foot. 'Is 'ee catchin' us?' Ginger's voice trembled as he got the words out. But I didn't dare look back. The hollow at the foot of the hill drew nearer. In another moment we had crossed it and were on our backs gasping for breath. A quick glance told us that the farmer had given up on us and retreated. He knew that once we reached the woods he would have no chance, and he now stood where we had been moments before, inspecting the damage to his wheat.

He had vanished by the time we recovered. I watched him until his head disappeared over the horizon. 'Ee's gone,' I murmured absently. Ginger raised himself on an elbow to have a look. 'Ee didn't scare me,' he said. For a few moments we lay motionless on the grass gazing up at the sun. Finally, we parted company. They returned to South Hetton by a roundabout way, so as to avoid running into the farmer, and I disappeared into the woods and began the long hike home.

After the war, miners got first one, then two weeks holiday with pay. Some people spent their holidays at home. It was said of certain men, in jest, though with more than a hint of truth, that they spent their holidays at the club. But it was usual for families to pack a few sandwiches and enjoy odd days out at the seaside. Mam and Dad loved the seaside, especially the sea air, so we made the most of it whenever we had good weather. Mam would make up some egg and tomato sandwiches, and Joseph and I would pack our towels and bathing costumes and take along a bucket and spade for Kevin. Then we would get the bus to Sunderland, after which a tram or Corporation bus would take us over the Wearmouth Bridge to Seaburn.

An advert for the twin resorts of Roker and Seaburn.

Once we had gotten used to the temperature of the sea, Joseph and I were happy to spend hours splashing about in the shallow water, or exploring the rock pools. We left the water only when we felt hungry, to eat our sandwiches and to take long draughts of the fizzy pop that Dad bought from one of the shops on the sea front. Warmed by the sun, Mam and Dad would happily contemplate sand and sea from the depths of their hired deck chairs. After a while, Mam would take out her knitting; while the needles click clicked away, Dad smoked his pipe, and kept an eye on Kevin, who would be contentedly building his sand castles, before demolishing them in sudden fits of destructiveness. About mid afternoon, Dad would go to Notariani's on the top for ice creams; cornets for us children and sandwiches for Mam and himself. Vera and Albert often joined us on these outings, bringing along their family, Albert junior, who was a couple of years younger than Joseph, and Gerard, who was then a toddler.

Our two families once joined a coach trip to Redcar. I especially liked Redcar because it had an indoor swimming baths on the sea front. It

Aunty Vera, Uncle Albert and young Albert.

The Independent Methodist Chapel Trip to South Shields. Included are: Annie Armstrong, Lilie Dobie, Annie Purvis, Marion Purvis, Mollie Coxon and Mrs Greenfield.

was a warm day, and the town was thronged with day trippers. As it became time to leave the beach behind us and make our way to where the coach was parked, all the Murton folk assembled on the promenade, where began an impromptu concert. From Barney Adamson's mouth organ the notes of a popular tune filled the air, and soon one of the Lashley twins was playing the spoons in accompaniment. In a moment of spontaneity, two men sprang forward from the crowd and began to entertain the assembly with their energetic and intuitive dancing. Spurred on by rhythmic hand-clapping, they quickened their steps. Some of the women, with engaging lack of reserve, shrieked uproariously. From where we were seated on a little ornamental wall, Joseph, young Albert and myself observed the performance, faintly bewildered, but enjoying every minute of it.

Passers-by had to step off the pavement and into the road to avoid the crush. They paused long enough to cast an amused eye over the proceedings and to shake their heads indulgently before moving on. A conservatively-dressed, middle-aged couple lingered near where we were sitting and the woman smiled at the three of us good-naturedly. Pointing to the two Murton men cavorting on the pavement to the extemporary sound of mouth organ and spoons, she said something to her companion. 'Oh, they're pitmen and their families,' the man said, with a faint grin, adding knowingly, 'Those people are like that.'

A packed beach at Crimdon. The beaches of the North East attracted many local holidaymakers in the years before and after the Second World War.

The mood prevailed throughout the return journey, sustained by a few loud and tireless extroverts. An hilarious exchange of anecdotes among a mixed group of men and women at the front of the bus was producing howls of laughter, and clearly winning the battle over Barney's mouth organ. Anyone wishing for a quiet, restful time, perhaps nursing a hope of getting their head down, must have been disappointed. We were about five miles from home, when a bald, thickset man went round with a cap inquiring 'Anything for the driver?' The men then searched their pockets for coins, generously selecting only the silver ones, before dropping them into the cap. There was nobody who didn't put in, and by the time every man on the bus had contributed, the cap was sagging with the weight of coins. Once the money had been counted and handed over, the bald, thickset man who had done the collecting made a brief announcement: 'Ladies and Gentlemen, the collection for the driver amounted to two pounds, eight shillings and sixpence, and he thanks you all very kindly.' Then everyone murmured their satisfaction that the collection had reached a respectable total. When the coach pulled up on the edge of the Cornfield, we alighted, feeling rather jaded and, after shouted goodbyes and with Dad carrying Kevin, who by this time was sound asleep, walked the short distance home.

Redcar was a favourite destination for the old people's annual trip. This left early in the morning and returned in the evening, and more than twenty coaches would be used for transportation to and from their destination. A carnival atmosphere awaited their return, as a large crowd massed by the roadside at the bottom of the Terrace, and the colliery brass band prepared to give them a rousing welcome home. The foremost coach would just come into view along the Waterworks road, when someone on the margin of the crowd would call loudly, 'Here they come!'; then the bandmaster would raise his arms into a horizontal position, baton at the ready, and the bandsmen would raise their instruments to their lips and their eyes to the baton. Glancing back over his shoulder, the bandmaster would wait until the first of the coaches appeared in Murton Street, then the baton would come down and the loud, brassy notes of the band would combine to fill the air with some lively tune or other. As each coach rounded the bend at the Colliery Inn and proceeded up the Terrace, the crowd would wave and cheer loudly, and the old men and women would wave back through the windows of the coaches. All along the route home, from the top of the Terrace past the Temperance Club and skirting the edge of the Cornfield, people stopped to wave, until finally the coaches pulled up at the Old People's bungalows, where, with parting shouts and much laughter, their occupants slowly disembarked, after having taken up the customary collection for the driver, of course.

A group from Murton at Blackpool in 1950 – George Coxon (driver), Billy Purvis, Marion Purvis and Annie Purvis.

Mam and Dad had friends who lived on Walney Island, off Barrow-in-Furness, where Mam had lived and worked as a young woman, and the summer of 1947 began a long sequence of yearly holidays when we went nowhere else.

Barrow seemed to me like the other end of the world, probably because it was on the opposite coast and took so long to get there. We rose with the larks on the day of departure, and with Dad carrying the two full-size suitcases, made our way to Murton station for the early train to Sunderland. After changing trains at Sunderland, we soon after arrived at Newcastle Station, where Dad enquired about our connection to Carlisle. Dad could never relax until we were safely on the train, and was always hurrying us along. 'Be quick, all of you,' he would snap, hurling the words over his shoulder, as he raced ahead with the suitcases. 'Over the bridge. It leaves in ten minutes.' And he would be waiting impatiently at the open door of the railway compartment until we stragglers caught up. From Newcastle to Carlisle was a slow journey, and must have made numerous stops, because it took about two hours to complete. They were steam trains, of course, noisier than modern trains, and dirtier; if you opened a window, you could be rather sooty by the time you had reached the end of the line. As the wheels flew over the rails, they made a rhythmic sound, which I imitated by tapping the window ledge of the compartment with my fingers. The rhythm stuck in the memory and was easy to put words to – 'we'll soon be there, not long to go, not long to go ...'

Murton Railway Station – the starting point of our journey to Walney Island.

Mam and Dad on holiday – this time at Butlins, Filey, 1951.

The instant we alighted at Carlisle, Dad would be on the go again, hastening from one platform to the next ahead of us, checking time-tables, checking his watch, chiding us for not keeping up – 'Come on! Platform two. We haven't much time.'

Mam, carrying her coat and her own little bag, would get exasperated. 'Jimmy, I'm not running. We're in good time for the train. Anyone would think you were in a race.'

Carlisle to Carnforth was another wearisome two-hour train ride; but the last stage, Carnforth to Barrow, was much more agreeable. The rail

Joseph and Kevin.

track roughly followed the shoreline of Morecambe Bay, stopping every few minutes at small, coastal stations with romantic-sounding names – Arnside, Grange-over-Sands, Cartmel, Ulverston, Dalton-in-Furness. Usually, the platforms of these stations were deserted; we stopped long enough for the odd passenger to get on or off the train; then the doors would be slammed shut, the guard would blow his whistle, and we would be off again. Finally, after arriving at Barrow, a short bus ride across the town's two bridges, passing the Vickers-Armstrong shipyards, brought us to the charming island of Walney. The journey, from leaving home to arriving at Black Butts Lane on Walney, took a whole day; today, travelling by car, I imagine it could be done in little more than two hours.

The old people's trip was one of two events which took place every summer and which exemplified, each in its own way, the special solidarity of Durham pit folk. The other event was the Durham Miners' Gala. Durham Big Meeting, as it has always been known locally, was a vast working-class pageant and the largest trade union gathering in the world, which could trace its origins well back into the 19th century.

Early on the morning of the big day, the lodge banner would be unfurled and paraded through the streets before departure for Durham, preceded by the colliery band, and accompanied by miners' union officials and numerous hangers-on, both the serious minded and the jovially eccentric, of whom every colliery had its quota. Prancing about in comical fashion, sometimes rigged-out like pantomime dames, they could be counted on to enliven the occasion; for the Big Meeting was never a staid affair.

The scene in Durham was unforgettable, as more than a quarter of a million people crowded the twisting thoroughfares of the old city. They pressed forward slowly but purposefully, laughing, dancing, some linking arms to form chorus lines in advance of band and banner. From Elvet Bridge up Old Elvet towards the racecourse was one tumultuous mass of seething humanity. As each banner passed before the County Hotel, and the strains of the band carried upwards, the invited guests – union leaders and Labour Party heavyweights – waved cheerily to the entourage from the balcony above. The colourful, richly symbolic, banners commonly depicted heroes of the labour movement, such as Keir Hardie and Peter Lee, and bore slogans like 'Unity is Strength'; some were draped in black, denoting that a fatality had occurred at the

The Dawdon Lodge Banner crosses Elvet Bridge on Big Meeting Day.

pit in the year leading up to the Big Meeting. It was a test of stamina for the VIP guests, for it was hours before the last lodge banner was carried aloft past the County Hotel.

Later, they would deliver their speeches before thousands on the racecourse. But politics were far from the minds of many people. Families happily picnicked on the grass, while those eager to go boating on the river joined the queues which formed by the water's edge. Many were drawn to the fairground amusements, where a Wurlitzer might be heard pounding out its cheerful notes in competition with the odd bandsman practising only feet away. For some, the rush and clamour of the gala had given over to a tranquil, worshipful mood, and they made their way to the great Norman Cathedral, which, together with Durham's ancient castle, dominated the city from the escarpment high above the Wear.

The Murton Lodge Banner at the Miners' Gala in later years.

At the end of the day, the banner was brought home to Murton, and for the second time paraded through the village, an event which created a fair amount of excitement, for it brought throngs of people from their houses out on to the street. 'I can hear the band!' someone would cry eagerly, while it was still some considerable way off. Then, after a few moments, 'I can see the banner!' Eyes would be strained for a glimpse of it coming into view above the heads of the crowd. In a short while, the parade would go by, the band playing a rousing march, people walking proudly in procession behind the banner, children skipping along at the side, the two men bearing the weight of the poles which supported the banner by this time feeling the strain and sweating profusely. The parade concluded with a march down the Terrace to the Miners' Hall at the bottom, where the procession disbanded, and the lodge banner was carefully put away until the next time.

Murton Colliery Prize Band on a postcard sponsored by OXO.

Summer nights could be light until ten o'clock, so I was rarely in the house before that time. Quite often, I walked up to Hill Crescent at the top of the Cornfield to call on Paddy Doyle and Joe Riley, who lived in adjacent houses, and Arthur Crane, who lived around the corner from them, and who, like them, was in my class at school. Only a ten minute walk away, was a favourite haunt of ours known as the Watergate. The Watergate was a marshy area near where the stream which ran through Willey's fields and the dene bubbled up from its source below ground. Sprawling unconcernedly in a hedge, we contemplated the sky and reflected on things like friendship and loyalty. When the philosophical mood had passed, we filled our clay pipes with dried leaves or tobacco from cigarette ends and tried to smoke them. Though we feigned enjoyment, the stuff tasted awful, and our pipes soon went out; but none of us had the money to buy pipe tobacco.

Occasionally, we would light a fire on the Cornfield and roast taties. Outdoor fires gave rise to a great sense of camaraderie among boys, who would sit around them for hours, talking amongst themselves. The taties would be placed among the white ash at the centre of the fire and left until they were cooked; then they would be retrieved from the fire with pointed sticks and, after a bit of hand-to-hand juggling, carefully skinned and eaten. It was impossible to wipe them completely clean, so if, like me, you relished the skin, you had to eat your tatie seasoned with wood ash. Mam always knew when I had been near a wood fire. Immediately I walked in the door, I would get it in the ear. 'Where have you been? Your clothes stink of smoke.' Then I would be made to have a good wash before going to bed, and my clothes would be bundled up and thrown in the laundry basket for the wash.

For summer evening diversion, nothing could match the sheer novelty and crowd-pulling potential of the button shows. For one brief, colourful interlude in the year, the bottom of the Cornfield resembled a fairground, as people set out their stalls and punters flocked around with their bags of buttons.

Anyone could have a button stall: a few magazines folded to about six inches square, and a half-brick to mark the distance from which the button had to be thrown, and you were in business. The most common prizes were boys and girls weeklies, children's comics and old books. If you could throw a button so that it landed on the prize without bouncing off, then the prize was yours. Enterprising girls would set out stalls with purses and handbags that had once belonged to their mothers and elder sisters. Not infrequently, such things found their way onto a button stall without the previous owner's knowledge or consent.

In no time at all, button show mania would sweep through the neighbourhood. Virtually no house remained unaffected by it. Every household kept an assortment of buttons for future use in the sewing box or in a special button tin. Adults complained when these were found to be empty. When someone's pyjamas or Sunday shirt required that the odd button be replaced, none could be found. In a quite unique exhibition of collective insanity, buttons became a more valuable currency than money itself. In some, the phenomenon approached the seriousness of an addiction. Jack Radestock incurred the wrath of his mother and had to flee the house after he cut all the buttons off his new suit before he had had the opportunity to wear it. The fever eventually abated, however, and sanity was restored, as the summer wore on and the onset of the dark nights put paid to the button shows for another year.

HIGHS AND LOWS

Good times in Murton – the Independent Methodists' members and friends in the Miners' Hall in the 1930s. Included are: Tom Simpson, Esther Tilley, Ethel Simpson, Susie Tilley and Eva Huntley.

I was twelve years old when the German children came to live in Murton. There were about thirty of them, all of primary school age; each was found a home with a local family, becoming, for the three months of their stay, an integral part of that family. I am not sure how the idea originated, but a German-born woman who lived in our street and who took one of the children had something to do with it. Ours was one of the families that participated in the scheme; so for a brief interlude in the summer of 1949, Mam got the little girl she had always wanted.

It was shortly after dusk when she returned home with Ruth. Ruth was not in the least shy, as one might expect of a small girl newly-arrived in a foreign country, but outgoing. She was a little older than Joseph – a week after her arrival, she celebrated her ninth birthday – and she endeared herself to us at once by her unabashed and gregarious nature. Ruth was of a robust build, so her tomboyish ways, evidenced throughout the forthcoming weeks, seemed perfectly natural to her. She wasn't especially pretty, but she had an impish smile that befitted her spirited character, at the same time revealing a slight gap between her two front teeth. Her near-straight, shoulder-length hair was a shade of blonde which, after long hours in the sun, appeared almost white.

Communicating with her wasn't as difficult as we might have expected: we pointed to ourselves and to one another and pronounced our names, and she sounded them and remembered them, and we followed the same procedure with objects. We also found other ways of conveying our meaning – by pulling a face and saying the word 'bad', for example. Ruth was keen to learn, repeating with evident pleasure whatever words we could come up with and that were suggested to us by the proximity of things or the practicality of the situation, and she

The family with Ruth in 1949.

would tell us their German equivalents. She told us that her name was Wagner, and that she hated fish, because where she lived fishing was a major industry and she could never escape the smell of it. She was very bright. By the end of that first night, she had already acquired quite a vocabulary of English words; within two weeks, she was speaking in sentences.

That first evening stretched out until quite late, by which time it felt as though we had known Ruth for ages. Mam had taken to her right off, and though Dad rarely showed his feelings, there was no doubt that he felt the same way. When it came time for bed, Mam showed her to her room and helped her unpack.

The following day, the Germans were given an introduction to an English school. Since they went to school with the children of the family they were staying with, Ruth was among the dozen or so who attended St Joseph's. She and I parted company at nine o' clock that morning and I didn't see her again until four, when Big Gal took a roll call outside of all the German children, together with their English 'brothers' and 'sisters'. Under the gaze of a hundred pairs of eyes, many of them openly mocking, we were paired off and lined up in a single column with Ruth and myself at the head. Then, to my intense embarrassment, Big Gal made us walk hand-in-hand down the school yard and out the gates.

Such cissified hand-holding I considered detrimental to my image, so immediately we were out of sight of the school, I broke it off, but, being loathe to hurt Ruth's feelings, in a less than obvious way, letting my hand fall casually to my side as though forgetful of its existence. Mindful of Mam's injunction not to loiter, I went directly home, with Ruth tagging along by my side. Our Joseph, who I thought got off very lightly in the matter, fell in with his friends and made his own way home.

On Saturday, an improvised football match took place on the Sea View ground at Cornwall, involving a team drawn from among the German visitors and one made up of local boys of the same age. Sea View was the last street in Cornwall; beyond it lay a wide expanse of rough, uncultivated land. On a largely stony surface, with only the odd patch of grass here and there, a football pitch had been marked out and completed with iron goal posts, though without nets. The pitch was regularly used for schools' football. The game was arranged in the friendliest of spirits and was the first of many events to be staged for the mutual benefit of visitors and hosts.

After some understandable reticence on the part of the Germans, the ice was eventually broken and henceforth everyone got on famously. They seemed in most respects hardly different from the rest of us, except that they spoke a different language and had names like Franz and Fritz and Otto. There was one noticeable difference with regard to appearance, though. The girls, some of whom were very pretty, were dressed as ordinarily we were used to seeing girls dress, and practically indistinguishable from their English counterparts. The boys, however, stood out: the short trousers that boys of my own age customarily wore came to just above the knee; but those worn by the Germans were micro short, exposing the full length of their thighs, and making them appear distinctly effeminate, an impression that was soon dispelled directly the Germans took to the football field. One of the boys was wearing lederhosen, an unfamiliar garb which previously I had only seen in illustrations for books like *Heidi*.

Not all our visitors were avid footballers; once they had picked their team, they were found to be two players short, so, to even the sides, the two best Murton players assumed German nationality for the duration of the game. A lot of people turned up to watch, and to throng the touchlines and the area behind the goalposts. Very sportingly, they gave the Germans great vocal encouragement; everyone, excepting those playing for the local side, seemed to want the visitors to win. They were strong competitors, and at the end of the game ran out winners by the odd goal in seven.

The presence of the German children, and the good times we shared through organized jaunts and entertainments, gave rise to a quite unique community spirit, not only between them and us, but also between all those who took them in and made them welcome. As a result, lasting friendships were formed among local people, many of whom had had only the most fleeting contact formerly.

At school, Mr Conroy, a new teacher, was successful in communicating his enthusiasm for Irish dancing to many among the senior pupils, who found the novelty of it appealing. Having first organized a team from among the senior girls, he then turned to the pupils of his own class to put together a mixed group of dancers, of which I was one. Every lunch break, we went across to the church hall, where we practised Irish reels in time to the, rather scratchy, music emanating from Mr Conroy's portable gramophone. The quaintness of the hall's interior structure, and the fact that we bobbed up and down a lot when we danced, meant that we were obliged to confine our dance routines to the small area of the floor at the centre, to avoid hitting our heads against the pitched ceiling. Nevertheless, after many weeks of practice, the entire dance troupe, seniors and juniors, was deemed good enough to appear before paying customers. Thus it was arranged for the Murton public to be given the benefit of a demonstration of our talents, to be performed on stage in the Rex cinema.

The practice of putting on a show accorded with a long-standing musical tradition in Murton and in pit villages generally, where there was never any dearth of voice coaches, piano teachers, tap and ballet instructors and the like. Concerts were staged yearly to showcase the pupils' talents and, parents especially, but also members of the general public, were always generous in their support. Dramatic societies, too, were popular, and many music teachers were also qualified drama coaches. A favourite form of entertainment was the Review, which combined choral numbers and dance routines with the performance of a one-act play. The plays typically depicted scenes of, supposed, working- class domesticity. They featured stock characters like hen-pecked husbands, put-upon wives and harassed fathers of teenage girls, who all spoke with exaggerated northern accents and dropped their aitches and put aitches where they shouldn't be, and were about as representative of the working-class as Bertie Wooster was the upper class.

The Miners' Hall was the usual venue for such performances. Built in the mid 1870s, during a boom in building activity which also saw the emergence of Cornwall, Holy Trinity Church and the Terrace, it was designed as an all-purpose social centre for miners and their families. Every pit village had a Miners' Hall. Murton Miners' Hall had a stage at one end and a gallery at the other, which was rarely used as it was considered unsafe. The floor was used for dances, though it was unsprung and hard on the feet.

The cover of one of the plays performed by the Murton Drama Club.

A cutting from the Seaham Weekly News.

For the performance of musical and dramatic entertainments, benches were put in and the dance floor became an auditorium. Back stage, a long passage opened on to a number of rooms, which were used for political and miners' union meetings, as well as for more leisurely activities such as whist drives, and pie and pea suppers. During the presentation of stage shows, they became dressing rooms for the performers.

Many amateur singers and actors found an outlet for their talents in the Amateur Operatic Society, an institution familiar all over the North East, with the pitman's love of music, and a cultural improvement to any pit village large enough to support one. Some operatic societies were of a near professional standard, and the Murton company was known to be one of the best. Names spring easily to mind, and those of an older generation will recall people like Ralph and Lydia Ridley, Harry Tweedy, Sheila Kirby among many others, who were mainstays of the company. The principal comedy role always went to Harry Wills, a gifted comic actor who, it is easy to believe, could have made his reputation on the professional stage, but who instead spent his working life underground. Rehearsals were held all year round for shows such as *Rio Rita*, *Rose Marie*, *Nina Rosa* and *The Lilac Domino*, for operettas often took their names from the principal female character.

The Amateurs always gave their performances in the Rex, which could hold more than five times as many people as the Miners' Hall. Moreover, the Rex had a wide, deep stage, with ample room in the wings, and an orchestra pit; the dressing rooms at the rear were connected to the wings at each side by a flight of stone steps. The show always ran for six nights. You could get a seat anywhere on Monday night, for that was the night of the first performance after the dress rehearsal the day before, and people reasoned that if mistakes were to be made they would more than likely occur on the first night. For the remaining nights, the show was always well attended, and every seat in the house would be booked for the final performance on Saturday night.

Few other companies could attract the number of customers sufficient to fill the Rex. It was with some sense of apprehensiveness, then, that the St Joseph's Irish dance troupe waited in the wings while preparing to demonstrate their four-hand, six-hand and eight-hand reels. We had rehearsed our complex dance movements over and over within the confined area of the church hall, performing them to the, not always melodious, notes of Mr Conroy's gramophone records; now we were to perform them on the spacious stage of the Rex cinema, and to the accompaniment of a live orchestra. Mam and Dad came to the performance, bringing Ruth with them, and there was a near full house when the lights dimmed and we stepped out on to the stage. We rather surprised ourselves when everything seemed to come together exactly as we had hoped it would, and confidence increased with every step that we took. In fact, it was probably the best that we had ever performed. It was an unprecedented thrill to hear the applause ring out at the conclusion of the performance.

More talented performers – Cold Hesledon Women's Institute Choir. Lily Richardson, the pianist, is second from the left in the front row. Norman Barker, in the middle, was the conductor.

While I was involved with the Irish dancing, someone in authority had decreed that an inter-schools athletics meeting should take place at the grammar school at Wingate. It was the first and only inter-schools athletics meeting that I had any knowledge of. So when I wasn't occupied practising six-hand reels in the church hall, I was concentrating my efforts on the school playing field, vying with others for a place on the athletics team.

Ours was the smallest school taking part, and we were up against some very powerful opposition. Being one of the youngest hopefuls, my options were limited. I didn't impress when throwing the cricket ball, being considerably younger than Harry Irons and Nicky Jobe, who were both selected for this event, and was also too young for the tug-of-war side. I was a poor sprinter, slow off the mark and often last to finish. However, I excelled at jumping events, especially the high jump, and rather presumptuously, if not unreasonably, I allowed myself to think that my selection for one of these events was a formality. On being informed that my name was on the team sheet, my presumption seemed justified. I was less than thrilled on learning that, instead of competing as expected in one of the jumping events, my sole responsibility would be that of running the first leg of a sprint relay.

Wingate was no more than eight miles away to the south, but nobody had ever been there. It was easier to go by rail, for in those pre-Dr Beeching days it was possible to take a train to almost anywhere. So early on the morning of the athletics meeting, the southbound platform of Murton Village Station overflowed with an excitable, chattering throng of adolescents such as it had never witnessed before, as the St

Joseph's crowd mingled with the considerably larger contingent of athletes from the Council School, who also were competing.

The grammar school buildings at Wingate ran parallel to the main road running through the village, and faced on to the sports field where the track and field events were to take place. The margins of the field were crowded with pupils from the various schools taking part; their teachers wandered around carrying clipboards and looking frustrated. I sat on the grass with the rest of our group and watched the proceedings with interest.

When the time came for the sprint relay, I joined the other runners on the track. The loud speaker crackled loudly before an adult voice issued the command, 'On your marks', signifying that the race was about to start. I got down on all fours along with the rest. 'Get set,' boomed the loud speaker. I tensed my body and waited for the crack of the starting pistol. Immediately it was heard, the person in front of me sprang forward and began to disappear down the track. I gave chase, with not the faintest hope of catching him, but giving it everything I had. Then I heard the sound of heavy feet pounding the track and someone from behind tore past me like an express train. I seemed almost to be standing still, though I was straining every muscle and sprinting at the top of my ability. I finished my leg trailing the rest. A chorus of adult voices from the edge of the track exclaimed 'Well done!', in exaggerated tones, and their owners applauded me warmly as I left the track dejectedly.

I had managed to hand over the baton without mishap, an achievement in itself, but giving my colleague on the second leg a lot of ground to make up. The St Joseph's team came last, a result that was to be repeated with depressing regularity throughout the afternoon. Thankfully, the Council School fared much better, ending the day in either first or second place overall, thereby ensuring that the reputation of Murton suffered no disgrace.

A class from Murton Junior Mixed School, with their teacher Mrs Robson, in 1950. Pupils from Murton Secondary School joined us at the sports day at Wingate.

Since most of our athletes competed only once, we were spectators for the other events. The day was warm and sunny and, despite our school's poor showing, we enjoyed ourselves. At the end, everybody went indoors, where we were given mugs of hot chocolate served from huge urns, the first time I had had hot chocolate as distinct from cocoa, and plates of biscuits were put out for us to help ourselves. The prizes were then given out, and everyone applauded enthusiastically as the winners came forward to accept them. Our school may have ended up with the wooden spoon, but I hardly think there was anyone present who wasn't glad that we had taken part.

After weeks spent living amongst us, and the accumulation of a rich store of mutual and affectionate memories, the day dawned when our visitors had to pack up and return to their homes in Germany. It was doubtless a joyous time for the families who awaited their return, but it was a sad day all round in Murton. I can only imagine how heart-rending it must have been for Mam and Dad when Ruth departed. Having her live in our home as one of us had enriched all our lives. Joseph was the same age as Ruth; like Dad, he didn't show his feelings much, but if he was making an heroic effort not to cry, he wasn't the only one.

Ruth and I didn't always get on: we had played together a lot, but there were times when we had fought, as brothers and sisters do. During one particularly acrimonious quarrel, I hit her over the head with my cricket bat, which got me into serious trouble with Dad. Now that the time had come for parting, I was reminded of these disagreements in an agonised pang of self-recriminating regret.

Sometime after midday, I said goodbye to Ruth and left for school, knowing that when I returned home she would be gone. I felt wretched. Who knows what emotions Ruth herself was enduring. My feeling of wretchedness was hardly ameliorated, but rather compounded, when on arriving at school I was informed by Miss Robinson, who had succeeded the now-departed Mr Conroy, that I was being dropped from the Irish dancing team.

Ruth's family was not affluent, and when she arrived in Murton she was not all that well off for clothes. Throughout the three months of her stay, Mam made sure that she wanted for nothing, and when she returned home to Germany she did so rigged out with a full wardrobe of new clothes. She and Mam corresponded for many years, and Mam sent her things at Christmas and for birthdays. Our German neighbour translated her letters for us, for although Ruth had become a fluent English speaker, she wrote only in German.

Not long after the departure of the German children, my grandparents moved into one of the old people's bungalows in Barnes Road, which was not too far from where we lived. The farm cottage at Fatten Pasture which had been their home for many years was out of the way, on the fringe of Murton; now they were practically living on the doorstep. A walk to the top of the Cornfield covered more than half the distance between our house and theirs.

Granda Slater didn't live long after they moved, dying barely a month short of his seventy-fifth birthday. This was then considered an advanced age. He had stomach cancer, and in the later stages of the disease was confined to his bed. Mam and Vera spent a great deal of time at the house throughout the course of his illness, but it was Mam's misfortune to be absent when he died. She was in the kitchen with Joseph and myself when a small boy from the street who had been inveigled into performing the function of messenger by either Vera or my grandmother, arrived with the news. He barely got the words out – 'Mrs Slater sent me to tell you that your father has died' – when Mam fled to the sitting room in tears and prostrated herself before a statue of the Child of Prague. Joseph and I knew enough to leave her alone.

I probably learnt more about my grandfather when he was on his death bed than at any other time. He had always been a private man. He practised his religion in a quiet, unobtrusive way, and if he thought deeply on any subject, there were few who were privy to his thoughts. His bed lay against the wall in a corner of the room. Throughout the last weeks of his life, he kept his eyes riveted to a crucifix which hung from the side wall, and obstinately refused to lie in any other position.

My grandmother was on her own for twelve years after my grandfather died. The delivery of concessionary coals that was Dad's entitlement was more than ample for our needs, so Dad arranged for every second load to be dropped at Grandma's house; then Dad and I went to the house to put it in. When our load arrived at our own house, we did the same. Where we now lived, we lacked the advantage of a coalhouse and hatch adjacent to the street, and the coals had to be carried along the front path in pails to the coalhouse, which, instead of being separated from the house, was now an extension of it. Dad and I used an old tin bath, which we carried between us, together with a pail each, which we clutched in our free hand. The bath was worth a dozen pails, but by the time we had swept up, the job still took us forty or fifty minutes. Grandma's house was situated even worse than ours, for there the coals had to be carried down the garden path and around three sides of the house to the coalhouse at the rear. Once the coals had been put in, it was a relief to know that it would be several weeks before another load was due.

Grandma was never short of visitors. Vera and Albert now lived in a council house conveniently close to where Grandma lived. Being a keen gardener, Albert kept her well supplied with vegetables and fresh flowers. He was still working at Thompson's Red Stamp Stores, and called in daily on his way home from work. When a branch of the Co-op Store opened at the end of Barnes Road, Grandma got her groceries from there. It became my practice to call from school every Friday after four to do her shopping for her. I take no credit for that, however, as it wasn't my idea but was done on Dad's insistence.

WINTER

Murton WI Children's Christmas Party in 1949. Included are: Mrs Ellison, Miss Dustan, Lily Simpson, Brenda Wallace, Sybil Ord, Rita Wallace, Albert Scothern, Kenny Dixon, Joan Richardson, Ann Simpson, Myra Ellison, Joan Simpson and Judith Ord.

A Harvest Festival in Dalton-le-Dale Church. On the ladder is Jenny Olaman with her mother, Mrs Wilson, below her. Ann Simpson is third from the left.

By early Autumn, field and hedgerow begin to look distinctly drab. The cereal crops have been harvested, reducing acres of land to stubble, and ubiquitous late bloomers like willowherb and knapweed are fast fading from view. Skies take on a metallic blue or silver aspect, in which the sun is no more than a pale disk, lacking all warmth; and you begin to be conscious of the coolness of the air against your cheek, not cold exactly, only you weren't aware of it before.

After blackberrying time, many people became engaged in seasonal farm work. This took place over two weeks in October, during which time the potato crop was harvested. The event coincided with the school holidays, so they were always known as the tatie-pickin' holidays. The labourers were mostly boys and girls of thirteen years and upwards. There were few who could resist the opportunity of working out of doors on a farm, and the remuneration at the end of the week was an added incentive. For two consecutive years, I worked for old Mr Cooper of Slingly Hill Farm, picking potatoes in the field next to the lower field where the wartime aircraft had crashed.

Disillusionment quickly followed upon my first day's experience, as it was painfully borne home to me that farmwork was no great fun, and that tatie-pickin' in particular was harsh, unrelenting labour that brought no time for open-air relaxation. Rising early on those crisp, Autumn mornings and tramping the mile and a bit to Cooper's farm to face a full day's work in the fields was a routine I looked forward to with ever-decreasing enthusiasm. Only the camaraderie that developed among the pickers to some extent offset the back-breaking drudgery of the work.

Shortly after dawn, I met up with my fellow labourers at some point en route to the farm. Everyone was dressed in old clothing, variously coloured but uniformly warm. We assembled at the farm house, still rubbing the sleep from our eyes and with the feel of the blankets still around us, and hoisted ourselves on to the trailer behind the tractor, which was to take us to the field where the potato crop was waiting to be picked.

The workforce was strung out across the field from end to end, and everyone was appointed a strip on which to work, and given a number of baskets to fill. The strips were paced out and set apart by having sticks stuck into the ground about a dozen furrows back. As the work proceeded, and one after another the furrows disappeared, the sticks were moved further back. Each time the tractor passed along the row, the ploughshare unearthed scores of potatoes, scattering them over a wide area. Once the baskets had been filled, they were collected and then emptied into a high-sided trailer, and the empty baskets thrown back. The time it took to pick a strip clean of potatoes seemed to have been worked out with mathematical precision. Every circuit, I worked like fury to pick my stretch and fill the baskets, before collapsing into the next furrow for what I hoped would be a few seconds respite, only to hear the imminent approach of the tractor beginning its next circumnavigation of the field. No matter how quickly I set about scooping up the potatoes, I could never do better than keep pace with the tractor, the sound of which I grew to hate.

At lunch time, we devoured our sandwiches eagerly, impervious to the smell of earth and tractor oil. Of the others who toiled alongside me in the field, I knew most if only slightly. The adults were unknown to me, but a bond soon developed between them and us. They said amusing things which made us laugh, and kept our spirits up, making the long hours bearable. I made new friends in Lance Forster and Jack 'Pussy' Southeran, and the three of us spent our lunch breaks sprawling between the furrows or lying on our backs on the compact, tyre-marked earth, where the tractor had passed and where, a short while before, potatoes had grown.

By the end of the week, I ached in places where I had never ached before; but I was mindful of an unaccustomed feeling of satisfaction that came with the knowledge that I had done a job of work and done it well. At the end of the week, everyone was paid; it was more money than I had ever seen before. When I got home, I proudly handed over my earnings to my mother, and was allowed to keep an amount which far exceeded my regular weekly pocket money.

Jack and Lance being equally flush, the three of us celebrated with a visit to the pictures, stopping first at Stobie's sweet shop, where, money being no object, we indulged our taste for sarsaparilla tablets, liquorice torpedoes, sherbet centres and whatever else took our fancy. We bought tickets for the adult seats in the Empire, and made pigs of ourselves throughout the performance. Jack left his seat before the end without a word of explanation and didn't return. At first, I thought he had gone to the toilet, and then when it became obvious that he wouldn't be coming back, that he had found the big picture boring and gone home. Lance, who had been sitting next to him, could offer no reason for Jack's abrupt departure. When the lights went up at the end of the show, we saw the reason: Jack had been sick all over the floor.

As the dark nights descended and November 5th approached, I went out at night with Mosey from the street, knocking on doors to ask politely, 'Please, can you spare a penny for the guy?' November 5th celebrations engaged whole families, and bonfires and firework displays were to be seen in every part of Murton. But for the youth of Murton, it was no more than the culmination of events. The pleasure gained in collecting wood and watching the bonfire grow day

Two lasses working hard in the tatie fields.

by day was too tame and unadventurous for adolescents with a proclivity for more robust amusements, and the greatest fun to be obtained during Autumn nights came from the practice of raiding neighbouring bonfires, a kind of juvenile gang warfare. Street gangs, often fifty or more strong, would descend with savage shrieks upon the bonfire of a rival territory in a determined bid to capture it, to be met and engaged in rough combat, by those who were equally determined on defending it. To come away with a tree or a log seized in the skirmish was a minor victory; if, by superior numbers or the element of surprise, the whole bonfire could be carried off, then not only was a crushing defeat inflicted upon a rival street gang, but the size of one's own bonfire was thereby significantly increased.

Our great rivals came from Hill Crescent, which looked down on Toft from the top end of the Cornfield. The two bonfires were sited in clear view at respective ends of the field, and being a mere five hundred yards apart, were invitingly close. Because an attack could be launched from Hill Crescent at any time, our bonfire had to be well guarded. Some of the houses in the street, including Mosey's, had a flat-roofed outhouse, comprising a coalhouse, a washhouse, and a lavatory. Mosey hit upon the bright idea of safeguarding the bonfire by storing it on the roof until November 5th, when, it was proposed, everyone should help in removing it to the Cornfield, where, at the appropriate time, it would be lit. Mosey's mother grumbled a little at first, but the plan went ahead. By climbing an adjoining fence, anyone agile enough could pull himself up on to the roof of the outhouse; the materials for the bonfire would then be passed up from below. Fencing, old clothes posts, sleepers, pallets, wooden crates and boxes, bits of old furniture, mattresses and the odd hawthorn tree, cut and dragged from a nearby wood, went on to the roof, and were pressed down to make room for more. Even after Mrs Littlejohn moaned about it being an eyesore, and Mr Littlejohn complained that the rain was adding to the weight, we hardly slackened in our efforts, and the mountain of timber on the outhouse roof grew by the day. Every day, Mosey was congratulated on the brilliance of his idea, and Mosey swelled with justifiable pride.

Then, one day, Mr Littlejohn was sitting on the outhouse lavatory reading his newspaper, as was his habit, when with a sudden accelerated rumble reminiscent of the coal bunker dropping a load of coal, the roof came in on top of him. Thus did the brilliant idea come to ruin, as was immediately deduced by Mosey and myself, who were sitting on the outhouse back step at the time. Had we doubted it, from behind the lavatory door a long sequence of raking coughs followed by an even longer, and, for Mr Littlejohn, wholly uncharacteristic, sequence of expletives spelt it out with a finality impossible to misconstrue.

Once Mr Littlejohn's temper had cooled and it was safe enough to approach, Mosey and I were obliged to remove the bonfire to the field bit by bit, and then to sweep out the outhouse. It took us two hours before the work was completed. When the bonfire was erected in the Cornfield, everyone in the street was amazed at how huge it was. We bragged amongst ourselves that it was the biggest bonfire Murton had ever seen. The following night, we got careless and left it unguarded, and the Hill Crescent lads swooped down from the top of the Cornfield and cleaned us out.

At certain times, late in the year, the clouds would grow dark and heavy, and the temperature would drop so that the cold pinched your mouth and nose. Then, caught up by icy draughts and blown haphazardly, the first flakes of snow would fall to earth, skittering on pavement and road. On cold December nights after a heavy snowfall, a busy traffic would build up outside as eager youngsters took to the streets with their winter sledges.

With woollen gloves for my hands, a balaclava to keep my head and ears warm, and a muffler tucked into my jersey, I managed to withstand the cold well enough. Girls were similarly protected; heavy muffled, with thick leggings beneath skirt and coat, and their faces glowing under tam-o-shanters. Every winter, Mam bought me riding breeches; they laced up at the bottoms, and the stockings were then pulled up over them and folded back, so that they protected the legs against the cold. Your clothes did still get wet; lying full stretch on sledges that were only inches off the ground made it unavoidable, and you couldn't escape the slush thrown up by passing sledges. Sometimes ice particles found their way inside your clothing, which could be discomforting for a moment, until they melted.

The biggest crowds were drawn to a street separating Ripon Terrace and Harrogate Terrace, and running parallel to the Rex cinema. Many considered it the best place in Murton for sledging. The street was steepest near the top, and continued to fall away until the last house had been passed; the sledge would then shoot off the end of the road, landing, after a three foot drop, in the Demi field, where it was brought to a halt by deep snow.

Some sat upright on the sledge, but most preferred to lie belly down in the belief that it made the sledge go faster. Occasionally in the run up, someone would stumble and the sledge would get away from them and go careering off until it reached the bottom of the bank, necessitating a long walk to retrieve it, accompanied by not inconsiderable risk, as sledges would be flashing past every few seconds. Trains were formed by linking two or more sledges together, those lying face down at the rear hanging on to the runners of the sledge in front. You had to be alert walking back, so as to avoid having your feet taken from under you and being carried to the bottom sprawled atop of someone else, who may or may not have been amused.

The countdown to Christmas, like the approach of the summer holidays, had that same sense of heightened anticipation. In church and in school, the advent hymns of promise such as *Jesus! Thou art Coming, Holy as Thou Art*, gave way to the well-loved Christmas hymns. At no other time in the school year did St Joseph's pupils require so little prompting to make them sing, or did the corridor and classrooms echo to such fervent singing.

On the Friday afternoon before we broke up for Christmas, lessons were suspended, and Christmas parties took place in every classroom. The cakes and foodstuffs we took to school were pooled, and we were allowed to bring games from home and to sit with our friends. One time, we held our Christmas party in the church hall and Fr Conway walked in on us as we were taking it in turns to sing songs around the piano. After praising our efforts, he suggested, as a novel departure from musical tradition, a croaking contest. Producing a half-crown from his trouser pocket, he offered it as a prize for anyone who could best croak a song, While others hesitated, I rose to the challenge. By constricting the throat muscles and lowering my voice to the level of my boots, so that I sounded something like a Jimmy Durante recording accidentally set at low speed, I croaked an exaggeratedly hoarse rendition of *If I Had My Way*. Father led the applause at the end, and I pocketed the half-crown.

There was never a more joyous sound than when the bell went at four o'clock to signal the end of the school term. Everybody loitered on the way home, reluctant to part company, and more than usually loquacious, keen to prolong that feeling of breaking up for Christmas.

The community at large shared in the anticipation. The Terrace shops, festive bright and tinsely, exuded Christmas cheer, especially after dusk, when the shop lights were on. Buses to Sunderland departed from the Store Clock crammed with Christmas shoppers. On Saturdays the twenty minute service was hardly adequate, so the bus company was forced to put on extra buses. People commonly bemoaned the fact that Sunderland was crowded and the shops too busy to be able to shop in comfort. But if they wanted that special Christmas gift, to Sunderland they were obliged to go.

Night time brought the opportunity to go, heavily muffled against the cold, around the doors singing Christmas carols. Usually we went in twos, but sometimes we ventured out in greater numbers, and the extra carollers gave a greater resonance to the singing. From a repertoire familiar to all of us through long practice, we gave every householder the benefit of at least three carols, solemnly rendered, followed by the cheery ditty, *We Wish You a Merry Christmas*, and ended with the spoken request, 'Can you help the carol singers, please?' We waited patiently until the door was opened, accepted gratefully the money offered, said 'Thank you' and left. At the end of the night, we doled out our takings in equal shares.

An advert for Joplings of Sunderland from the 1930s.

The Store Clock – Murton's familiar landmark.

Christmas morning was the only morning when Joseph, Kevin and myself were early risers by choice, and we would usually be squatting in the middle of the living room floor surrounded by our presents when Mam and Dad came downstairs. We could each count one main present – a train set, perhaps, or a fort and tin soldiers – and there would usually be a paint box, possibly a torch, and, always, a book. Stockings were emptied first, though their contents varied very little from one year to the next. Typically, there would be an exercise book, pencils and a rubber, crayons, a ball, and an apple and an orange; the remaining space would be stuffed with assorted nuts.

Christmas morning allowed no more than a prefatory enjoyment of presents, for soon these had to be put to one side as it became time to get ready for church. As on a Sunday morning, the first Mass of Christmas morning was the 9.00 am Mass (realistically, 9.20 am). Strictly speaking, Midnight Mass was the first Mass of Christmas, but none of us attended Midnight Mass until after we had left school, and Mam and Dad never.

There was a special atmosphere about Christmas morning Mass. The choir was always in excellent voice – Jimmy Rankin had been rehearsing it for weeks – and there wasn't anyone in the congregation who didn't join in the singing. Fr Conway, in his brief sermon, would remind us of the reason for our presence at church, and conclude by wishing everyone present a happy and a holy Christmas. After Mass was over, he customarily shook hands with his altar boys before retiring to his presbytery for breakfast.

It took a while for the church to clear, as people queued at the front, eager to view the Christmas crib. They thronged the churchyard outside, smiling greetings, and proffering warm handshakes and heartfelt wishes. 'Merry Christmas.' 'Many of them.' 'The same to you.' The mid-morning air echoed to the sound of season's greetings, and for a while nobody showed any inclination to leave. Schoolfriends all had the same question on their lips – 'What did you get for Christmas?' And each endeavoured to outdo the other in reply.

The streets would normally be quiet save for the odd, solitary figure hastening to pub or club, who would greet us with a hearty 'Merry Christmas,' when we would eagerly reciprocate. The colliery band, on its routine tour of the village, could be heard when periodically it stopped to render a few carols. After completing its itinerary, the band customarily repaired either to the Demi or Big Club, both of which would be plentifully decked out for the season and full to overflowing. There, the Christmas Day drinkers would be given the benefit of some festive musical cheer, and, doubtless, after the recital many of the band members themselves would down a celebratory drink or two.

As it was Christmas morning, Mam would cook a breakfast of bacon and eggs. Dad gratefully tucked in; as for the rest of us, breakfast was usually bolted down, for we were preoccupied with other things, and, if the day was fine and dry, keen to call on our friends. Having a late breakfast meant that, unavoidably, Christmas dinner was late too, and

Mam spent the next couple of hours preparing it. Dad did his bit in washing and drying the breakfast dishes and peeling the vegetables for dinner, before departing for the Demi. He left with Mam's full approval. Though Mam never drank herself, she was outspoken in defence of the rights of others, especially men, to indulge. Many men found consolation from the unremitting grind of pit work in pub or club, and she knew this. 'A man works hard and should have a drink,' was her curt response to those advocating temperance.

The Demi Club and, left, Steward's House, with St Joseph's Presbytery and Holy Trinity Church in the background.

Dad arrived back just in time to carve the bird before Mam put the dinner on the table. From out of the dining room window, we would spy him approaching, striding out over the rugged slope of the Cornfield, his regular short-cut home. After a couple of hours at the club, Dad would grow expansive, quite often waggish, especially with Mam; sometimes, when he came close, I caught the pleasant whiff of beer on his breath.

Christmas dinner was like Sunday dinner, only with extras. There were the customary new potatoes and green vegetables, and, of course, the endless supply of Yorkshire puddings, without which no Sunday dinner or Christmas dinner would be complete; in addition, there were crisp, roast potatoes, lightly seasoned stuffing, and sauces to complement the chicken or goose, traditionally preferred to the normal Sunday joint. To follow, there was Christmas pudding, dark and fruity, with white sauce or custard that covered it and came up to the rim of the dish.

Vera and Albert came with their family for tea, and while they were alive, my grandparents came too. Mam put on a big spread, with savouries and cakes, jelly and cream, and traditional mince pies. The Christmas cake, which Mam always made and iced herself, was cut into for the first time, and toasts were made and reciprocated with sherry or ginger wine, which, though it burned the throat as it went down, was a great favourite of mine. Later, we played cards and board games and snacked on mixed nuts and raisins; we talked until it grew late, and it would be well after eleven before the company left for home.

Mam, Aunt Elsie, Vera and Albert in old age.

On New Year's Day, we went to their house, where we were entertained in lavish style, in what was a last, convivial echo of Christmas. Otherwise, I never cared for the New Year; it seemed a depressing anti-climax after the joys of Christmas. It was followed by a barren two months, which often brought the worst weather of the winter. My birthday in February formed a kind of oasis, and was a prelude to the spring.

Celebrations in Murton of a different kind on New Year's Day. This scene was Vesting Day on 1st January 1947 – the day when the mining industry was nationalised.

THE TOP CLASS

As I got older, sport played a bigger part in my life and like many who grew up in a pit village I loved football. Here is a great team from Murton. This Colliery Welfare football team was very successful in the 1930s – winning the Wearside League Championship in 1936-37 and the Monkwearmouth Charity Cup in 1934-35 and 1935-36 seasons.

Having failed the eleven plus, I stayed on at St Joseph's for the remainder of my schooling, eventually entering the top class where I was taught by Big Gal.

Big Gal's classroom was the most pleasant in the whole school. One window overlooked the blacksmith's shop and the Demi field. The window behind the teacher's desk faced south east, where the view was dominated by Batter Law Hill, an iron-age hill fort and prominent local landmark, and, on the lower slope of the hill, Wembley housing estate, built in the 1920s at the same time as Wembley Stadium. This eye-catching landscape was the cause of endless lapses into daydreaming, for which I was constantly having to be reprimanded.

The time spent in Big Gal's class meant that I got to know her pretty well; and with the familiarity that came of regular association, came also the realization that she was never quite as fearsome as she had seemed when, in the lower part of the school, my contacts with her had been few and random. So long as you kept your head down and concentrated on your work without daydreaming, talking out of turn, or otherwise wilfully distracting others, it was possible to get on with her. Big Gal didn't pull hair, or rant and rave, and only rarely resorted to the use of the cane, but controlled her class by the sheer force of her personality.

We had some fun with Big Gal. Hyperbole is a trait commonly found in the conversation of Northern pit folk, especially within the context of humour. Big Gal, by contrast, alternately puzzled and amused us by displaying a distinct tendency to underestimation, which, rightly or wrongly, we put down to her Irishness.

She was going through the routine of marking our English Composition books one day. It was Eddy Ganning's turn, and he was standing at her desk. Every few seconds she would mutter 'Huh!' in a sceptical tone of voice, and Eddy was beginning to look distinctly uncomfortable. Suddenly she had everyone's attention. 'Arnold Gruthious six feet tall! Huh! None of you have ever seen a man who was six feet tall.'

Eddy looked nonplussed, while quite a few incredulous glances were cast around the class. Everyone present knew of several people in Murton who were considerably over six feet tall, including Fr Conway and, possibly, Big Gal herself.

Linda Clarkson put her hand up. 'Please, Miss, Our Lord was the only man in history who was exactly six feet tall.'

'Nonsense!' came the crushing reply. 'That's a legend. No one knows how tall he was.'

After a while, something else in Eddy's composition piqued her interest. 'Go on. You've never walked a mile in your life,' she said, taking her eyes off the book and fixing Eddy with a look part scornful, part amused. Eddy was adamant that he had. 'Do you ...' she began. 'Does anyone have any idea how far a mile is?'

There was a moment's silence. 'Please, Miss, between the Waterworks and Murton Station,' I said, proffering an estimate at least twice the distance, for I had myself but the vaguest idea of distances.

She thought about it for a moment. 'Yes, that's a mile,' she agreed, then added, with a mischievous glint in her eye, 'In Ireland, we'd call it half a mile.' No one could say that Big Gal lacked a sense of humour, or that she didn't occasionally indulge in a little leg-pulling at our expense.

I had been in her class a few months when, one afternoon while the girls were doing needlework with another teacher, the boys were marched over to the school garden behind the church, ostensibly for nature study. Once there, I was handed a spade and told to turn the soil over at a patch of garden adjacent to the graveyard. Big Gal, meanwhile, busied herself tending plants in another part of the garden, where she attracted a small cluster of green-fingered students, to whom she happily dispensed advice.

I liked a well-kept garden but did not have green fingers myself, so I set to work with the spade, though without much enthusiasm. I had barely progressed beyond half a row, when I heard my name being spoken in a muted voice. I looked about and could see nothing at first, until I glanced over towards a row of poplars not ten feet away on the fringe of the garden, where, between the low-lying branches, I beheld Tommy Gilroy's head and neck sticking up above the level of the ground. He was resting on his spade, five feet down a newly-dug grave. Seeing my surprise, Tommy broke into one of his characteristic rattling laughs. I immediately shot an anxious glance at Big Gal, but she had her arms full of plants, and was explaining something to Billy Atkinson, and too engrossed to notice.

Tommy heaved a sigh. 'Aa didn't feel much like comin' to work this mornin,' Pat,' he said wearily, and I knew one of Tommy's jokes was coming. 'Aa was drinkin' in the Demi last night with Jack Sharkey and Mick Smith,' Tommy continued in his matter-of-fact way. 'At the end of the night, we reckoned up, see, and Jack had spent one pound two shillings, Mick had spent one pound and eighteen pence, and Aa spent –' Here Tommy paused pointedly '– one of the best nights Aa've ever had in me life.' Tommy's laughter crackled like a rapid burst of machine-gun fire, and, tickled as much by Tommy as by the joke, I doubled up, laughing as loudly he was. This time, the laughter was too loud not to be overheard. As Big Gal swivelled her head round, Tommy promptly disappeared into the grave, and I, and the wholly innocent Hughie Grogan, who was turning the soil a few feet away from me, were subjected to a tongue-lashing for slacking and indulging in trifling conversation. After buckling down to the work, I could still hear Tommy chuckling away to himself in the grave.

Big Gal had her own garden, attached to the bungalow she shared with Little Gal in a pleasant part of Murton Village. In addition to gardening, her spare time interests extended to cookery, which she taught to adults in the evening, so her talents were many and varied. She was also capable of rare acts of kindness. We were once required to produce a scrap book on the subject of our choice. I found a magazine at home with pictures of the lakes of Killarney. By simply cutting out the pictures and copying the captions, I was able to fill a scrap book with minimal effort.

There came a moment when we were asked to name our chosen topic. The predictable subjects were reeled off – footballers, film stars, fashion etc. I had recently committed some misdemeanour or other and was in her bad books, so there was a scornful edge to her voice when she came to me. I had decided to call my topic 'The Irish Countryside,' and proudly announced the title, confident that I had hit upon a more original choice of subject. She seemed taken aback, and, after she had gotten over her surprise, pleased. After the class had been set to work, she came and stood over me, offering advice about the project, and generally extolling the charms of her native country. For a whole week, she called me by my first name, until the commission of another misdemeanour landed me back in her bad books.

Every now and then, the school made a show of imitating the traditions of other schools. Once, at some time in my ten years at the school, we had a sports day, and once, when I was in the top class, we had a prize-giving day. Actually, it was held in the afternoon, and lasted about an hour.

Once it had begun, I relaxed, and settled into the role of spectator. Unfortunately, I was a mathematical duffer. I was good at art, but there were at least three in the class who were better than me. I was probably the second best at English; however, Rose Hart, who wrote highly literate and imaginative stories, was the clear favourite for the English prize. The end of the proceedings drew near, and I must have been daydreaming for I was startled to hear my name announced. She was standing at the front of the class holding a copy of Rider Haggard's *Eric Brighteyes*, and looking at me. Inside the front cover, she had written: 'Prize for best scrap book, presented by M. Gallagher. Christmas, 1950.' The prize was obviously an afterthought. It wasn't a new book and so must have come from her own bookshelf, which, in a way, made it more worth having. It is still in my possession.

Big Gal must have liked poetry, for she had us commit whole chunks of it to memory. I was not greatly enthusiastic about it myself, and was not alone in that respect, but, unlike some, I had the ability to memorize it fairly quickly, so poetry lessons became tolerable, if less than inspiring.

We were introduced to Shakespeare when one term the class began a study of *Julius Caesar*. It was a very limited study, in that we managed to learn only one speech, but drama was a new venture for us. Almost new. In Mr Conroy's class, we had been encouraged to indulge in creative role play. Mr Conroy was fresh out of Teacher Training College, and doubtless imbued with new and fashionable ideas. Billy Atkinson and I were obliged to sit on chairs at the front of the class and told to imagine we were strangers in a railway carriage and to strike up a conversation. After a few pleasantries had been exchanged, like 'Care for a Craven A?' and 'Would you like to see some pictures of my wife and children?' the conversation fell flat. No one else fared any better, and this venture into the experimental theatre wasn't repeated.

Big Gal strove resolutely, in the face of stupendous indifference, to instil enthusiasm for *Julius Caesar*. We were instructed to read Cassius' speech, beginning with the words, 'I was born free as Caesar ...' which we did for the better part of a fortnight. Then came the time for the first reading before the class. Emily Gow was being inattentive and was caught out, so it fell to her to begin.

Emily Gow was a reader of excruciating slowness, whose mispronunciations were legendary. It was obvious that Shakespeare would give her problems. We waited expectantly.

Emily intoned: 'The troubled Tiber chaffing at her ...'

'Chafing,' came the correction. 'Chafing at her shores.'

'The troubled Tiber chafing at her shores ...'

A few sniggers were heard. They were silenced by a glare from Big Gal. 'We shall see in a moment if any of you can do better.' She paused, and all eyes returned to the text. 'Continue, Emily.'

'Upon the word, acc – accou –'

'Accoutred as I was.'

'Accoutred as I was ...'

Paddy Doyle shot his hand up. 'Please, Miss, what does accoutred mean?'

'It means he was burdened, weighed down with the equipment he was obliged to carry. Go on, Emily.'

'The torrent roared, and we did buff it with –'

'Buffet it.'

Emily looked blank.

'Buffet, not buff,' said Big Gal, her voice rising. 'You buff your shoes. Again.'

Still uncomprehending, Emily gave it another go. 'The torrent roared, and we did b-buff-et it, buffet it with lusty sine – sin – sine –'

'Lusty sinews!' roared Big Gal. 'We did buffet it with lusty sinews – oh, sit down, Girl!' She cast about the class and her eye fell on Linda Clarkson, sitting bolt upright, neat and pretty, and with 'pick me' written all over her. After such a disastrous start, Big Gal probably thought it best to give the nod to someone whose reading ability she could count on. 'Linda Clarkson.'

Linda stood up and held her copy of the play not quite at arms length. She smoothed her frock and gave a little cough. Linda was a good reader in that she knew all the words and paused in the right places, but her delivery had all the passion of a weather report. 'He had a fever when he was in Spain,' she said matter-of-factly. 'And when the fit was on him, I did mark how he did shake: tis true, this God did shake.'

The words fell from her lips, borne by a pleasant, genteel voice that betrayed not a modicum of understanding, still less of feeling. Big Gal must have been groaning inwardly, longing to hear some spark of emotion, an inflexion of the voice, that would convey something of

Cassius' murderous envy.

Linda came to the bitter, hate-filled words that concluded the speech – 'Ye Gods, it doth amaze me a man of such a feeble temper should so get the start of the majestic world and bear the palm alone.' – and her intonation was that of a polite waitress informing a diner that the Coquilles Saint Jacques was off and wondering if Sir would have the Scallops in White Wine instead. After a triumphant glance at poor Emily, she sat primly down, confident that she at least had done the Bard proud.

Following my acting debut in the imaginary railway carriage, my only other appearance in school dramatics was in a Christmas entertainment which the school put on for parents and children. The contribution of our class was a playlet condensed from the first part of *A Christmas Carol*. I was chosen to play the role of meek Bob Cratchit. The only furniture was the teacher's desk; the high, old fashioned type with the raised top. The class register served as a ledger, and a hen's feather made an authentic-looking quill pen; these were the only props.

I had the fewest lines, as my scene with Scrooge was really only a preamble to the main drama, which highlighted the confrontation of Scrooge and the ghost of Marley. My brief, distinctly bland, performance was far outshone by Bobby Kerrison's wonderfully spooky Jacob Marley, and, especially, by Paddy Doyle's barnstorming performance as Scrooge. The role was well-suited to Paddy's flamboyant personality, and he made the most of it, to the point of embroidering it here and there, striding about the stage and banging his fist on the desk, thundering 'Bah! Humbug!' until even the parents at the front shrank back in trepidation. Unfortunately, the irascible miser went too far and thumped the desk so hard the inkwell jumped out and splattered several of the front row patrons with ink. Despite this mishap, the performance was well-received, and at the end of it the three actors modestly stepped forward and took their bows.

One of my classmates was Maurice Wallace, who lived in our street. In his last year at school, Maurice lost a lot of schooling through ill health. He was convalescing at home when one day Cliffy Nichols, Nicky Jobe and myself decided to pay him a visit during the dinner break from school.

Maurice was still confined to bed, though able to sit up, and the three of us, joined by Maurice's uncle, Ned Johnson, who lived with the family, sat by his bed and had an enjoyable time reminiscing about school and keeping Maurice updated on the latest pictures being shown at Murton's three

Three inseparable friends – Cliffy, Nicky Jobe and the author.

cinemas. It gave us a nice feeling to know that Maurice was being cheered up by our visit.

We were enjoying ourselves so much we failed to notice the time, until Ned remarked that we would practically have to run all the way back to school to be in time for afternoon lessons. There was a pause as an unspoken thought passed between us, before Nick gave voice to it. Once said, there was not a moment's hesitation as all three of us decided to give school a miss and spend the afternoon with Maurice.

The gravity of what we agreed to do can hardly be appreciated today, but at that time no one ever truanted from school, at any rate, not from St Joseph's School. It was the ultimate transgression, meriting the ultimate punishment – six strokes of the cane, and what was probably worse, the displeasure of our parents once they found out about it. So the three of us were well aware of what we were letting ourselves in for.

The next morning, an expectant hush descended upon Big Gal's classroom from the very first moment, and I was made aware of the many glances being cast in the direction of myself and the other two lawbreakers. They were mostly admiring glances from the girls, or so I chose to interpret them, but some of the lads were grinning sadistically, in anticipation of what lay in store for us. After she had marked the register, Big Gal raised her eyes to the class and paused, and for a moment I thought she was going to deal with the matter herself. Then, in an impassive tone of voice as though it were nothing out of the ordinary, she pronounced each of our names in turn and told us to report to Miss Riley's office.

All miscreants sent to Miss Riley's room for punishment were obliged to stand outside in the corridor until she deigned to deal with them. The waiting was part of the punishment. Accordingly, Cliffy, Nick and myself lined up outside her room in clear view of anyone entering the corridor, before Miss Riley motioned for us to enter.

Miss Riley's room was two steps up from the corridor; it was carpeted, with a large, office-type desk, and a couple of cupboards flush with the back wall; the window offered a fine view of the Colliery Welfare grounds and the First Wood. Miss Riley always behaved according to due legal process in requiring a statement for the defence, and in listening patiently while one was given. It gave the impression of fairness. She was used to hearing plausible-sounding recitals, fabricated in the hope of gaining an acquittal. When, however, she asked where the three of us had been the previous afternoon, we simply told the truth as the only option available to us. Three inseparable friends who were all present at school in the morning and all absent in the afternoon, was a detail that could not so easily be explained away. She eyed each one of us in turn, before silently and solemnly going to the cupboard where she kept her cane. Despite her moderate size, Miss Riley could lay it on hard, harder even than Big Gal, but I remain convinced to this day that the reason she gave us only two on each hand instead of the mandatory three, was because the three of us had been engaged in one of the Corporal Acts of Mercy when we truanted.

We left Miss Riley's office with bruised and stinging hands, but with magnified egos. The incident was the talk of the school, and the three of us were heroes in the eyes of many, so the adulation we received made the punishment more than worthwhile.

When Maurice recovered his health, the four of us regularly travelled together to Roker Park on Saturday afternoons to see Sunderland's home games. It cost sixpence to go through the turnstiles of the boys end; adults paid the full price of admission, nine pence in old money. At the time, Sunderland was known as the Bank of England club. The side brimmed with internationals, and players such as Trevor Ford, Ivor Broadis and Len Shackleton were household names.

A Sunderland team from 1951. Back row: Arthur Hudgell, Fred Hall, Bobby Robinson, Jack Hedley, Tommy McLain. Front row: Len Shackleton, Ivor Broadis, Arthur Wright, Trevor Ford, Billy Bingham and Len Duns.

It was shortly after the war ended that Dad decided I was old enough for my introduction to Roker Park. I have only the haziest recollection of the event, but apparently it was a dull game. Sunderland beat Leeds 1-0 and Leeds were relegated. Dad claimed, rather cynically, that Sunderland were trying their level best to keep Leeds up. Playing that day, were Len Duns, Eddie Burbanks, and goalkeeper, Johnny Mapson, three of the 1937 Cup-winning side. Mapson continued to play for Sunderland for many years. I obtained his autograph when one

Saturday I was on a tram on the way to the match and Mapson got on at the north end of Wearmouth Bridge, carrying his football boots. How times have changed.

Sunderland goalkeeper, Johnny Mapson, in action at Roker Park.

Where sporting facilities were concerned, St Joseph's was the poor relation of the Council School, which had a couple of playing fields of reasonable standard. St Joseph's playing field had an incline of about one in twelve. Running across the width of it gave the impression of having one leg shorter than the other, so all games were played along its length.

The field had another disadvantage: it was corrugated, a result of medieval serfs piling up the soil, effectively creating more land on which to grow their crops. The legacy was a field of deep troughs and narrow ridges. On this surface, football was more a game of chance than of skill. Cross-field passes defeated the purpose, as the ball was prone to hit a sloping surface and rebound into the path of an opposing player. Plumb in the centre of the field, someone had erected a wooden telegraph pole, which had to be dribbled around. At unexpected moments, it would loom dangerously, and anyone forgetful of its presence or not quick enough to dodge aside, ran the risk of being concussed. Sad to relate, it was the occasion of much profanity.

The game of cricket had its problems too. Charging up to the crease along the ridge, the bowler was always liable to lose direction and go sprawling down one side or the other; and it was only too easy to go over on an ankle. So stumps were invariably pitched in the valley. Such an arrangement required accurate bowling, as wayward deliveries tended to pitch on the slope and ricochet at head height towards the batsman taking stance in the trough. By chance, no one was ever killed or maimed, though the potential for a calamity of the sort was ever present. It was under such constraints that St Joseph's sportsmen laboured to improve their footballing and cricketing skills. Eton it was not.

The Council School played their football in the A division of the Sunderland and District Schools League. The A division was comprised of teams from the grammar schools and the big secondary modern schools. In the last season before the war, Murton Council had won both the league championship and the Cochrane Cup, the major cup competition for schools football. St Joseph's played in the D division, which was made up of the, generally much smaller, Catholic schools. However, for such a small school, St Joseph's produced a number of outstanding footballers. Pat Duffy was a tricky inside forward and St Joseph's top goalscorer, who was regularly picked for the Sunderland Boys team. The school also had a commanding centre half in Bernard Finan, who played both for Sunderland Boys and Durham County Boys, and who might easily have gone on to play professionally had he not joined the Salvatorians on leaving school and trained for the priesthood.

The side I played in did quite well in both league and cup competition, without ever actually winning anything. We came runners-up in the D division and runners-up in the Stewart Cup. Getting to the final of the Stewart Cup was an important achievement for such a small school, for the competition was open to all schools in the Sunderland area. After overcoming a strong side from a secondary modern in the semi-final, following a replay, we were drawn against another big school, Silksworth, in the Final. The game was played on a neutral ground on a bitterly cold evening, within spitting distance of the sea. It was a big affair for St Joseph's parish, and we had a lot of support. I take pleasure in recalling the team for that night, though it was the same team that played virtually unchanged for two seasons. In addition to me in goal, the other players were Jimmy Rutherford, Harry Morris, Derek Knox, Bobby Kerrison, Eddy Ganning, Billy Atkinson, Arthur Crane, Albert Swan, Norman Burns and Nicky Newton. We put up a tremendous fight, but Silksworth's superiority told in the end and they won by the only goal, scored late in the second half.

We got a resounding reception from our supporters when we climbed aboard the coach for the return journey; but it did little to assuage the feeling of disappointment after we had come so close to winning a cup. On the way home, Fr Conway got the driver to stop the coach outside Brunini's ice-cream shop, where he treated every member of the team to an ice-cream.

Fr Conway was well-known in Murton for his love of football. His presbytery overlooked the Colliery Welfare ground, and when Murton played their home games he could be found sitting in the stand watching the game with his, mainly non-Catholic, cronies. Non-Catholics called him the Catholic Father. At one time, he had a season ticket for Roker Park. I was then his senior schoolboy altar server, and he loaned it to me whenever Sunderland Boys had a home game.

St Joseph's football team, 1951. Back row, left to right: A. Crane, D. Knox, J. Rutherford, the author, E. Ganning, H. Morris. Front row: N. Newton, N. Burns, R. Kerrison (captain), A. Swan and W. Atkinson.

Loaning me his season ticket was just about the last favour he did for me. Fr Conway smoked, was overweight, and to the best of my knowledge never indulged in physical exercise. This must have put a strain on his heart; and, indeed, aged only fifty-six, he eventually succumbed to a heart attack. He had just sat down to dinner when he collapsed to the floor. A doctor was sent for but it was too late. A visiting priest knelt to minister to him as he breathed his last.

Presently, what was one of the better St Joseph's football teams broke up. The best players in the side were all a little older than me and left school at Christmas, whereas I had to remain at school for another term. Billy Atkinson, Jimmy Rutherford and Eddy Ganning all found work at the pit, and Norman Burns gained a job in the colliery office. Cliffy Nichols, Nicky Jobe and Paddy Doyle were also working at the pit. I was now the oldest and biggest pupil in the school. Fr Conway had suggested that I come out of goal to play centre-half and to captain the side, and this I did throughout my final school term. The team was fortunate in having a fine replacement goalkeeper in Billy Bruce, who, during my tenure between the goalposts had been too young to challenge for the position, but who now was to make the goalkeeper's jersey his own. But we were an emasculated side, dropping points against teams that we had always managed to beat in the past, and I don't recall us winning a single game that term.

When, finally, I turned fifteen and left school, I experienced a momentary feeling of elation, which, with hindsight, only seems naive, when any reasonable assessment of my prospects might have given cause for despondency. The thought of a lifetime of graft in the dark galleries of the pit held little charm, had I but realized it; and I embarked upon it with neither enthusiasm nor misgiving, but with a vague and rather sad sense of the inevitable.

Epilogue

In recent years, the Waterworks road has seen a marked increase in the volume of traffic, certain times of the year, December, for example, giving rise to lengthy tail-backs as cars arrive from all over the county and beyond. Their destination is a multi-acre site where once stood the Murton pit heap and aerial ropeway, and where now stands the Dalton Park Shopping Outlet.

I mention this fact as being one instance, though a quite striking one, illustrative of the general trend of change that has come over Murton in the more than fifty years since I began work at Murton pit. Although the community was moulded by the coal industry, its progressive transformation has not been entirely the result of the coal industry's demise. Advances in mass communication, the ease of travel, the impact of technology on children's games, and a hundred other things have also contributed. The chronicle of another childhood and of a time later than mine might contain descriptions of theme parks, pop concerts, holidays abroad; and alude to television, transistor radios, DVDs, computer games … but that would be for someone else to write.

Apprentices from Murton Colliery at Houghton training centre in the early 1950s. Left to right: Ken Rowe, Jack Chapman, Clive Rodgers, Mr Chicken (supervisor), Ken Sinclair and Jack Lashley. An era came to an end when Murton Colliery closed in 1991.

Murton folk certainly know how to enjoy themselves. A year after I started work at the pit it was a time of great celebration – the Coronation of Queen Elizabeth II. Here are two pictures of Doxford Terrace's Coronation Street Party.

The People's History

To receive a catalogue of our latest titles please send a
large stamped addressed envelope to:

The People's History Ltd
Suite 1
Byron House
Seaham Grange Business Park
Seaham
County Durham
SR7 0PY